How the Tea Party
Captured the GOP

How the Tea Party Captured the GOP

Insurgent Factions in American Politics

RACHEL M. BLUM

THE UNIVERSITY OF CHICAGO PRESS   CHICAGO AND LONDON

The University of Chicago Press, Chicago 60637 The University of Chicago Press, Ltd., London

© 2020 by The University of Chicago

Published 2020

29 28 27 26 25 24 23 22 21 20   1 2 3 4 5

ISBN-13: 978-0-226-68749-0 (cloth)
ISBN-13: 978-0-226-68752-0 (paper)
ISBN-13: 978-0-226-68766-7 (e-book)
DOI: https://doi.org/10.7208/chicago/9780226687667.001.0001

Library of Congress Cataloging-in-Publication Data

Names: Blum, Rachel M., author.
Title: How the Tea Party captured the GOP : insurgent factions in American politics / Rachel M. Blum.
Identifiers: LCCN 2020005313 | ISBN 9780226687490 (cloth) | ISBN 9780226687520 (paperback) | ISBN 9780226687667 (ebook)
Subjects: LCSH: Republican Party (U.S. : 1854–)—History—21st century. | Tea Party movement. | Populism—United States.
Classification: LCC JK2391.T43 B58 2020 | DDC 324.2734—dc23
LC record available at https://lccn.loc.gov/2020005313

FOR MY MENTOR, HANS NOEL, WHOSE SCHOLARLY EXAMPLE AND
CONFIDENCE IN MY ABILITIES MADE THIS PROJECT POSSIBLE

Contents

Preface

I became preoccupied with the Tea Party in the spring of 2012, following a trip to a rural area of southwest Virginia where I interviewed a dozen activists in the Mechanicsville and King William Tea Party groups. At the time, I had no intention of writing this book. My only goal was to do some firsthand research for a graduate seminar paper. Going into the interviews, I thought I knew what the activists would say. I was prepared for them to tell me how angry they were about Barack Obama's election and Obamacare, about government spending, and even about changing mores concerning conservative touchstones like traditional marriage. To my surprise, the activists were not particularly interested in discussing these issues. They continued to steer the interviews back to a different theme: their distrust of the Republican Party. This made no sense to me. Why did these conservatives—most of whom were life-long Republicans—possess so much animosity toward their own party that they would rather rail about "RINOs" (Republicans in name only) than about Obamacare? By the end of the day I had developed an inexplicable need to answer this question.

My interest in the Tea Party and its hostility toward the Republican Party went much deeper than I had initially been willing to admit. I had, in a way, been preparing to write on such a topic for most of my life. I was brought up in what is now known as the Christian Right. Shortly before I was born, my parents had become "born-again" Christians. During my childhood, they increasingly saw evangelical Christianity and the conservative politics that accompanied it as providing a blueprint for protecting their children from what they saw as the evils of popular culture. As my parents' involvement with the Christian Right deepened, my orbit of acceptable activities, beliefs, and individuals tightened. The rationale for these restrictions combined religion and politics in a manner that made the two indistinguishable.

The first time I remember being aware of a break between "us" (the true believers) and "them" (liberals and secularists) was at the age of five. My family had attended the same mainline Protestant church for as long as I could remember, and I had been enrolled in an affiliated Christian school since the age of three. Every Sunday we went to services at this church. Then, one Sunday, we did not. We went to a conservative Baptist church instead. My parents explained that we had to leave our old church because it had become too liberal. They had come to realize that the church supported the theory of evolution over that of a literal six-day creation. To make matters worse, the pastor had recently preached acceptance of homosexuality *and* praised the denomination's recent decision to ordain female pastors. Soon thereafter, my parents told me that I would no longer be attending school—any school. Our new church encouraged parents to homeschool their children to protect them from the liberal brainwashing machine that was the public education system. Christian schools were also suspect because they set up authority figures in a child's life other than their parents, whose authority was granted by God—something that would encourage rebellion down the road.

As if overnight, my entire life changed. I missed my friends and the energy of a traditional classroom, and I missed feeling normal. At first I missed "regular" school, but my parents explained that they were homeschooling me to protect me. From what? As our involvement in fundamentalist homeschooling circles deepened, I learned of the dangers of secularist public school teachers, liberal Christian school teachers, and worldly classmates. I learned that being taught at home was part of being a good Christian. Being a good Christian was important to me because it was the only way to avoid going to hell, and I was very scared of hell. And, at least to the adults I was around, someone's politics could also mean they were going to hell.

I learned to associate words like "secularist," "liberal," or "worldly" not with the state of a person's soul, but with their politics. For example, Democrats were liberals who were atheists, which meant they were going to hell. This logic extended to a variety of other people who, according to conservative personalities like James Dobson and Rush Limbaugh, had violated the Christian-Republican consensus. These included abortion advocates, LGBTQ people, those who had sex outside of marriage, weed smokers, welfare recipients, rebellious children, feminists, environmentalists, and people who wanted to reduce defense spending.

Once I reached my teens, I was in possession of what political scientists might call a constrained set of issue positions. I did not know what I believed, but I knew what I was supposed to believe. Every night at dinner, my father would ask me what had happened in politics that day. There were definitely wrong answers to this question. Through a series of trials and errors, I developed a sort of formula for producing the right answers: choose an event that involved a problematic group, and criticize the group based on their lack of adherence to Christian values or Republican Party dogma. My parents were pleased by my sycophancy, and in 2000 they rewarded it by signing me up as a volunteer for Republican political campaigns. A year later, they enrolled me in a Christian debate league for homeschoolers, in which the winner was whoever best applied the "Christian worldview" to policy resolutions.

This debate league became my ticket to college. In Christian homeschooling circles, higher education was generally regarded with suspicion. Thankfully, my parents were an exception in this regard. They wanted me to get a degree—an opportunity they had never had—but they were concerned about the brainwashing of liberal professors. The answer was Patrick Henry College (PHC), a conservative Christian liberal arts institution that catered to homeschooled students. It even offered scholarships for achievements in the Chrsitian homeschool debate league in which I participated. PHC had been founded in 2000 by Michael Farris, darling of the Christian Right and advocate for homeschooling and "parental rights." Although PHC was a small college (the student body hovered around three hundred) with strict rules, it was bursting with opportunities compared to the narrow orbit of home and church that I had occupied for most of my life. I took the debate scholarship, and I went.

It was at PHC that the connection between conservative Christianity and Republican politics, which I had understood implicitly for some time, was made explicit. The college aims to train students to influence American politics and culture, as expressed in its motto, "For Christ and for liberty." PHC's focus is in line with the handful of organizations also founded by Farris that still share its Purcellville, Virginia, campus: the Home School Legal Defense Association, which lobbies and litigates for the rights of homeschool families; Generation Joshua, which organizes homeschool students into teams of volunteers for Republi-

can campaigns; and ParentalRights.org, which advocates for a constitutional amendment protecting the right of parents to educate (i.e., homeschool) and discipline (i.e., use harsh methods of corporal punishment)
as they see fit. PHC encourages its students to volunteer and intern for
these organizations in preparation for future involvement in Republican
politics. Its end goal is to produce conservative Republican foot soldiers
who will occupy positions, ranging from congressional staff to the Supreme Court, in which they can advocate for the rights of conservative
Christians.

During the 2008 presidential election I was assigned, as were many
other students who wanted internship credit, to lead a group of Republican campaign volunteers for Generation Joshua. As one can imag-
ine, the student body of PHC took Obama's 2008 defeat of John Mc-
Cain hard, and many were still nursing their wounds when the Tea Party
emerged in early 2009. Although those at PHC shared the Tea Party's
distress about Obama's election, the Affordable Care Act, and corporate bailouts, the Tea Party received very little attention beyond mild derision. We (for I never gave the topic enough thought to have an opinion)
criticized the Tea Party for its lack of focus on social issues like abortion,
and for its strategic misstep in not working more closely with the Republican Party. The Tea Party was dismissed as a waste of energy. I certainly never imagined that I would eventually conduct interviews with
Tea Party activists, much less that I would write a book on the topic.

As I began pursuing my PhD (I was miraculously accepted into a
program at Georgetown despite my untraditional educational background), I wanted nothing to do with conservatism, religion, or party
politics. For the first time in my life I felt that I could develop my own
opinions and identity, which, it turned out, were wildly different from
those with which I had been raised. In fact, I was embarrassed about my
conservative political roots, and did my best to hide my past from my fel-
low graduate students. Then my professor assigned our graduate seminar an article on the Tea Party to read. To my dismay, I found myself
engaging—even disagreeing—with the article. I was scared to express
my opinions in class, lest I reveal too much about my background, so I
went to see the professor, Clyde Wilcox, during his office hours. I told
him that I thought the piece was tone-deaf to conservative politics, and
that I thought I could do a better job, but I was afraid of being branded
forever. Wilcox was sympathetic to my plight, relaying his own experience in pioneering research on the Christian Right. Then he gave me

a piece of advice that made this project possible. My degree from a no-name Christian conservative college would always be on my CV, he said. I could let academia hold it against me, or I could do a version of what his research had done with the Christian Right, using my background as a tool to explain something that was hard for most academics to approach: conservative activism.

That conversation sparked a research agenda that would occupy much of my attention for the next seven years. At first, interviewing activists felt like putting on a piece of clothing I had long outgrown, but I found that I still knew how to think and speak like a conservative. I was able to frame my questions in a way that prompted Tea Party activists to be frank about their beliefs without fearing that I would "twist their words" to make them seem like circus curiosities (something about which they were quite sensitive). Of course, many Tea Partiers used rhetoric that could only be described as racist, homophobic, misogynist, conspiracy-theoretical, extremist, and xenophobic. This much did not surprise me; it bore too many similarities to the us-versus-them outlook of the conservative activists among whom I had grown up. What I could not explain through reference to my experience with conservatism, however, was the Tea Party's deep-seated vitriol toward the Republican Party. The Christian Right had understood itself as a sort of faction in the Republican Party, but the two were in a friendly alliance, making and receiving concessions. The Tea Party, in contrast, was overtly hostile to the Republican Party, showing a willingness to undermine the party's electoral fortunes from within, in a way that seemed more akin to an insurgency than to an alliance.

I undertook the ensuing years of fieldwork, interviews, surveys, and methodological training with the aim of understanding the Tea Party's strategy and the reasons for it. My hope is that this book accurately portrays the message Tea Party activists sought to convey, that it illuminates some of the most confusing aspects of the Tea Party's strategy, and that it draws lessons from the Tea Party that reach beyond this episode to explain the relationship of factions to the parties and party systems in which they arise.

CHAPTER ONE

Introduction:
An Intraparty Insurgency

To reform government, we have to reform parties . . . we can't reform politics from the outside. The Tea Party is a unique, historical, grassroots effort standing side-by-side with the GOP and holding them accountable. . . . We're not rallying anymore. Instead, we're permeating the government. — Ron Wilcox, remarks at a meeting of the Northern Virginia Tea Party Patriots on May 13, 2013

At six in the evening on May 13, 2013, I slipped into the back room of a sports bar in Fairfax, Virginia. I was there for a meeting of the Northern Virginia Tea Party Patriots (NVTPP). This was not my first time at a meeting like this; having conducted a number of interviews with Tea Party activists, and having attended multiple meetings and protests, I was familiar with the general format. Most meetings involved a Bible study–style conversation about some policy or political event, mediated by the group's leader. This meeting was different. After leading the group in prayer and a recitation of the Pledge of Allegiance, Ron Wilcox, head of the NVTPP, declared the meeting a "convention training session" to help the Tea Party "game" the upcoming convention of the Republican Party of Virginia (RPV), which would decide its nominees for the 2013 statewide general election.

Wilcox then introduced a guest speaker, a member of the RPV State Central Committee who was sympathetic to the Tea Party's efforts. The speaker explained the ins and outs of the convention process, outlining the number of delegates who could be sent from each district and what to expect in the rounds of balloting at the convention. In his estimation, the Tea Party could reasonably expect to control one-third of the delegate slots, which would be enough to tip the convention in the Tea Party's favor.

Next, Wilcox handed members a report card from the Family Foundation of Virginia that ranked the Republican lieutenant governor and attorney general candidates on a scale of "most obviously evil" to "least harmful." Wilcox emphasized that the NVTPP was not officially endorsing this handout or any candidate, but he did encourage members to take the handout into consideration when choosing which candidates to support. This was a common strategy for Tea Party groups. Most such groups refrained from officially endorsing any one candidate in an attempt to remain neutral, but made their preferred choice plainly apparent. After a brief but lively discussion, the group converged on the candidates listed as "least harmful" on the Family Foundation's handout.[1]

The plan, Wilcox then explained, was simple: Tea Parties across the state, united by the Virginia Tea Party Patriots Federation (VATPPF), would designate members to attend the RPV convention as delegates. Although the Tea Party would not hold the majority of delegate slots, one-third of the delegates united behind a clear slate of candidates would be able to prevail over the other delegates, whose support was spread out over the remaining candidates. The Tea Partiers would vote for their candidates in round after round, until the other candidates dropped out and the Tea Party candidates emerged as the favorites. This, Wilcox noted, was why "conventions are better than primaries."[2]

The 2013 RPV convention went according to plan, with the Tea Party's candidates emerging as the Republican nominees.[3] These candidates were then handily defeated by Democrats in the general election, after meeting resistance from prominent Virginia Republicans for being too extreme.[4] Virginia Tea Partiers were not particularly bothered by this; they may have lost the general election, but they had been victorious in the their skirmish with the Republican Party.

Of course, this example only pertains to one election in one state. I include it here because the strategy used by the VATPPF in 2013—taking over the Republican Party from within—is key to understanding the Tea Party's outsized political influence. It is impossible to tell the story of the Republican Party in the early twenty-first century without discussing the Tea Party insurgency. The Tea Party left its mark not only on statewide elections, but also on the Republican Party's policy positions, strategy in primaries, leadership in the House of Representatives, and even presidential nominations.

Despite the Tea Party's sizable influence on political institutions from parties to Congress to the presidency—inasmuch as the Tea Party paved the way for Donald Trump—few have attempted to explain the Tea Party as anything more than a blip in politics as usual. This does not diminish the work done by earlier scholars to explain the psychological and ideological motivations of Tea Partiers, including Williamson and Skocpol's overview of ideological inconsistencies among activists, Parker and Barreto's use of the framework of reactionary conservatism to explain sympathizers' psychology, and Irwin and Morris's extension of the reactionary framework to characterize the digital homestyle of Tea Party legislators.[5] Although these accounts have explained certain aspects of the Tea Party in great detail, they have stopped short of asking whether, much less how, the Tea Party aligns with what we know about how US political parties operate.

There is little precedent, at least in the last several decades of increasingly polarized parties,[6] for an intraparty insurgency like the Tea Party. Tea Partiers were willing to contest Republican incumbents in primaries, even if this meant later losing the seats to Democrats. They had no qualms about pushing Republicans to oppose popular legislation or obstruct governmental operations, even if doing so would damage the party's reputation. These are not the kinds of things that party activists ought to be doing in an age of decisive, polarized parties, yet these were the Tea Party's signature strategies. It is this paradox—the Tea Party's zest for intraparty warfare in a system hitherto defined by the conflict between two relatively cohesive parties—that this book seeks to explain. I describe the Tea Party as an *insurgent* party faction, drawing out the reasons it adopted a contestational strategy and the impact of this strategy on party politics writ large. More generally, this book builds a framework of factions based on observations of how factions, and particularly the Tea Party, behave. As I explain, this framework will allow us to differentiate between a destabilizing faction like the Tea Party and the types of factions that routinely crop up within parties in support of a particular candidate or policy. In this vein, the next section provides a brief vignette of Tea Party behavior in two different electoral contests, which serves as context for the discussion of party factions that follows.

A Tale of Two Tea Parties

The Tea Party's electoral strategy was riddled with what seemed like contradictions. While its name contained the word "party," it never became a political party. Tea Partiers often claimed that they were working independently of the Republican Party, yet they nearly always ran as Republicans. The Tea Party mobilized in response to Obama's election and the passage of policies like Obamacare, but it focused its electoral energy on ousting *Republicans* from office by confronting established Republican candidates in primaries.

These contradictions raise a variety of questions. Why claim independence and then work through the Republican Party? One explanation is that Tea Partiers generally conceived of themselves as Republicans. If this is the case, how do we explain the Tea Party's preferred strategy of challenging established Republican candidates? Conversely, if Tea Partiers did not consider themselves Republicans, why did they run candidates using the Republican brand? Here, I use Ohio and Virginia—two states with active Tea Party networks but divergent electoral rules—to untangle some of the intricacies of the Tea Party's electoral strategy.

Virginia's laws make it very difficult for minor parties to compete in electoral contests. Much of this is accomplished through the state's high bar for official party recognition. To gain official recognition in any district, a party must have run a candidate who received at least 10 percent of that district's popular vote in the last election—something minor party candidates rarely achieve. Recognition matters, because only officially recognized parties receive automatic ballot access.[7] Unofficial parties can attempt to obtain ballot access through other means, namely a cumbersome process requiring ten thousand signatures (at least four hundred from each of its eleven congressional districts). In contrast, at least prior to 2013, Ohio operated under electoral rules that were extremely friendly to minor parties, offering them state recognition, low petition signature requirements for ballot access, and the option to hold statewide primaries.[8]

Tea Party groups in both states fielded a number of candidates in the 2010 midterm elections, but they did so in very different ways. In Virginia, most Tea Party candidates only possessed one viable way of getting on the ballot: running as a major party candidate. Virginia Tea Partiers thus pioneered the strategy of challenging Republican candidates in nominating contests for the Republican spot on the ballot, a strategy they continued to use in the election cycles that followed. Ohio Tea Partiers did *not* run any candidates as Republicans in 2010. Instead, they fielded their candidates as representatives of one of the minor parties (e.g., Libertarians, Independents, or Constitutionalists), contesting Republicans and Democrats alike in the general election. As the *Columbus Dispatch* reported of the spike in Libertarian candidacies in 2010, "Seemingly better organized and riding a wave of antigovernment sentiment fueled by a poor economy, rising deficits, and a national Tea Party movement, Libertarians want to harness the public's dissatisfaction with the two major parties to become a true force in Ohio politics."[9]

A visual breakdown of the different strategies employed by the Virginia and Ohio Tea Parties in the 2010 federal midterm elections can be seen in figure I.I.[10] Third-party candidates (almost exclusively Tea Partiers) ran in thirteen of Ohio's eighteen congressional districts. Only one district—John Boehner's former district, Ohio's Eighth—had a contested Republican primary.[11] In contrast, of Virginia's eleven congressional districts, five had contested Republican primaries, most with at least one

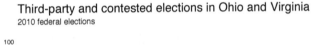

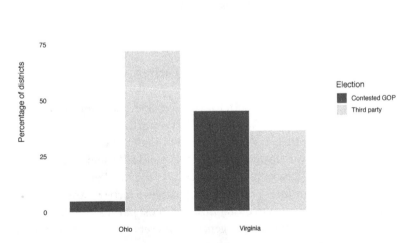

FIGURE I.I. Ohio and Virginia Tea Parties used different strategies for running candidates in 2010 in response to state-level electoral rules.

candidate who was affiliated with the Tea Party. The few minor party challenges that occurred in Virginia came not from the Tea Party, but from the state's affiliate of the Independence Party of America (called the Independent Green Party).[12] A mere four districts had Libertarian challengers, only one of whom (Stuart Bain) bore any residual relationship with the Tea Party.[13]

Many Ohio Republicans feared the Tea Party's continued exploitation of the state's electoral laws. In response, Republicans pushed for reforms to severely restricted ballot access for third-party candidates. These changes became law in 2013. The Libertarian, Constitution, and Green Parties of Ohio sued the state over these changes, and eventually lost.[14] After this point, the Ohio Tea Party adopted the insurgent strategy of Tea Partiers in Virginia and elsewhere.[15]

These vignettes show that as early as 2010, state-level Tea Party groups had begun to respond strategically to electoral barriers and incentives. The strategy of Ohio Tea Partiers in 2010 provides a rare glimpse of what the Tea Party might have looked like in a different electoral system: a minor party. Conversely, the infiltration strategy of the Tea Party in Virginia shows what that same political group looks like in a two-party context: a party faction. These examples suggest that the US two-party electoral system may breed a very particular type of faction: one that in a country with a multiparty electoral system would mobilize as a minor party, but which in the United States attempts to achieve electoral influence by infiltrating and taking over one of the two major parties.

Overview: The Tea Party as a Party Faction

In the following chapters, I offer a comprehensive account of the most recent insurgency in the Republican Party, treating the Tea Party as a party faction. But first, I offer a framework that allows us to differentiate factions from other ways of mobilizing politically, and to distinguish among different types of factions. I describe the Tea Party as a specific type of faction: an *insurgent faction*. Insurgent factions are characterized by their willingness to destabilize their host parties in order to seize control of them. Factional insurgencies represent one of two things: the reaction of a group or groups within a party to its perceived loss of dominance in that party's coalition, or the attempt of a previously nondominant group to wrest control of the party. In contrast to other types of factions, which generally cooperate in exchange for a seat at the table, insurgent factions are content with nothing short of obtaining a controlling interest in the party.

The Tea Party's Transition into a Faction

Of course, the Tea Party did not emerge in 2009 as a fully formed party faction. Early on, it was little more than a mood. The first widely acknowledged mention of the Tea Party as a contemporary phenomenon occurred as if by accident in what became known as the "Santelli Rant," a televised speech in which CNBC's Rick Santelli encouraged all "capitalists" to join him at a "Chicago Tea Party."[16] In the following months Tea Party rallies cropped up in locations from Oregon to Pennsylvania, culminating in the Tea Party Tax Day protests in Washington on April 15, 2009, which were advertised by Fox News and organized with help from inside-the-Beltway organizations such as FreedomWorks.[17]

By 2010, thousands of local Tea Party groups had formed around the country. Some of these were affiliates of national umbrella organizations like FreedomWorks, but most were independent, run by stay-at-home moms, retirees, and local business owners. These groups held monthly meetings, hosted speakers and candidate forums, participated in rallies, organized canvassing efforts, educated members about topics from Milton Friedman to the UN's Agenda 21, published blogs, and fleshed out the Tea Party's organizational apparatus.[18] These local Tea Party groups increasingly extended their criticisms beyond President Barack Obama to the Republican Party. Although local groups differed on the finer points, there was an emerging consensus that the Republican Party of George W. Bush was not going to stop the bevy of political changes occurring in America—at least not under the leadership that existed at the time.

The strong performance of Republicans in the 2010 midterm elections initially diverted attention from the Tea Party's budding factionalism. But a closer review of Tea Party activity in the months leading up to the 2010 midterms reveals Tea Party challenges in a variety of Republican primaries.[19] Some of the Tea Party's challengers were inexperienced or unviable, such as activist Christine O'Donnell, who challenged and defeated Republican veteran Mike Castle in Delaware's Senate race, only to lose the seat to the Democrat, Chris Coons, after an embarrassing episode of campaign ads in which she assured voters, "I'm not a witch."[20] But many Tea Party candidates fared better than O'Donnell—indeed, better than Republicans with no Tea Party affiliation—resulting in a sizable cohort of Tea Partiers among freshman Republican House members.[21]

In the following years, the Tea Party continued to employ insurgent tactics. From statewide contests, like the 2013 RPV convention mentioned at the beginning of this chapter, to high-profile upsets like local Tea Party favorite David Brat's defeat of House Majority Leader Eric Cantor in 2014, the Tea Party's electoral strategy involved opposing established Republicans, regardless of the cost. In the House of Representatives, Tea Party Republicans showed a penchant toward procedural radicalism, playing a key role in the 2011 and 2013 federal government shutdowns and eventually all but forcing John Boehner, the more moderate Republican speaker of the House, to resign. Through such insurgent operations in local, state, and national arenas, the Tea Party waged a war of attrition on the Republican Party. The result, with the 2016 nomination and election of Donald Trump, was a party whose voters were relatively receptive to messages of anti-elitism and the threat of outsiders—a party that was powerless to stop the nomination of Donald Trump, and whose members in Congress supported, or at least rarely opposed, President Trump's increasingly controversial policy proposals.[22]

What Is a Faction?

David Hume described factions as "types of rivalry."[23] Later, David Mayhew defined them as "organizations competing within a local party,"[24] Giovanni Sartori called them "specific power groups,"[25] and Daniel DiSalvo explained them as groups that aim to shift their parties along the right-left ideological spectrum.[26] These definitions leave us with the sense that factions are organized expressions of political rivalry. But in order to explain the Tea Party as a party faction—and an insurgent one at that—we need a definition that will help us to distinguish them from other groups within parties, and to differentiate among types of factions.

I argue that factions, at least in the United States, are an institutional response to a party system that leaves little room for electoral influence outside of the two major parties. Factions are subcoalitions of policy-demanding groups that in another electoral system would likely organize as minor parties. In a two-party system, these subcoalitions mobilize as miniature parties within a major party. These factions then attempt to undermine their host parties in order to gain control over the parties' agendas. The resulting tension is often misdiagnosed or ignored, making it difficult to identify factions when they emerge. This book builds on the definition of factions as miniature parties within parties to construct a framework of factions that will allow us to explain destabilizing episodes like the Tea Party, and to distinguish these from periods of coalitional cohesion. I structure this framework around three broad questions about where factions fit in the US political system.

First, how do factions differ from other policy-demanding groups within party coalitions? Parties are, after all, home to a variety of groups at any given time, many of which do not disturb the coalition's equilibrium. I explain factions as subcoalitions of fringe groups within parties that are willing to undermine those parties in order to increase their influence over the parties' agendas.

Second, what is the boundary that separates factions from other non-party political entities such as interest groups and social movements?[27] Although factions, interest groups, and social movements may overlap substantially, interest groups and social movements do not need parties in order to exist or to effect change. Factions, then, are unique in that they develop within parties, can only exist within parties, and seek change through parties.

Finally, do different types of factions exist in the US party system, and if so, how can we distinguish among them? The word "faction" is often used to describe a group that arises in an attempt to influence a party's stance on a specific issue, such as a candidate or a policy. As such, they tend to disappear after that candidate loses or the piece of legislation passes. I refer to these factions, which in a sense, are not factions at all, as *particularistic*. I contrast them with *programmatic factions*, which are sub-coalitions that seek to renegotiate their party's consensus on policy, its organization, or both. I divide programmatic factions into two categories based on the strategies they use to gain influence. *Consociational factions* attempt to broker power-sharing arrangements, while *insurgent factions* like the Tea Party rely on procedural radicalism and similar contestational strategies in an attempt to wrest control of the coalition.

To clarify these distinctions we can consider an example from the Democratic Party during the 2016 presidential nomination cycle. The

Democratic playing field quickly narrowed to two candidates: Hillary Clinton and Bernie Sanders. As the story goes, Clinton represented the established interests of the Democratic Party, whereas Sanders embodied a more progressive, even populist, vision for the party. Sanders's promises of free college and an end to corporate greed were particularly persuasive to younger white male voters, known as "Bernie Bros." The Bernie Bros certainly wanted something specific, and wanted it from their party: Bernie Sanders's nomination. Existing for this sole purpose and fading from Democratic politics with Sanders's loss, they could be thought of as a particularistic faction.

But Bernie Bros were not Sanders's only supporters. Sanders enjoyed backing from a more robust faction within the Democratic Party: the democratic socialists (sometimes referred to as the progressive *lane*).[28] Nor was Sanders the only representative of this faction. Two years later, democratic socialist Alexandria Ocasio-Cortez defeated ten-term Democratic incumbent Joe Crowley in a New York congressional primary. Understood in this way, the Bernie Bros, like the early Tea Party protesters, had been dancing on the surface of a larger programmatic faction all along. Inasmuch as Democratic Socialists' strategy involves contesting other Democrats in party primaries in exchange for electoral influence, they could even be described as insurgent, differing from the Tea Party mainly in that they seem to have possessed fewer means of wresting control of the coalition out of the hands of party regulars.

The Tea Party as an Insurgent Faction

At the beginning of this chapter, I relayed an anecdote from a meeting of the NVTPP, in which they developed a strategy for taking over the 2013 Virginia Republican nominating convention. This example illustrated important aspects of what it means to call the Tea Party an insurgent faction. It mobilized within and worked closely with the Republican Party *when such action was necessary for electoral success*, going so far as to co-opt many of the GOP's electoral structures. Further, Tea Partiers had no qualms about opposing established Republican candidates in primaries, even at the expense of losing those seats to Democrats.

Generally, insurgent factions are willing to take these risks because they hope to gain control of their party at all costs. Some insurgent factions seek to replace the party's old identity with a new one, as was the case with Barry Goldwater's New Right conservatives or even the contemporary democratic socialists. Other factions aim to rescue an older version of the party from the jaws of change. This latter motivation bears many similarities to the "reactionary style of conservatism" that has been shown to characterize the motivations of Tea Party sympathizers (and, more recently, of Trump supporters).[29] In short, Tea Partiers were reacting to what they perceived as too much change in "their" country and "their" party. They saw reclaiming their former dominance in the Republican Party as the best means of influencing political decisions that would reinstate their privileged status in "their" country as well.

The following chapter lays out a framework of factions. The next five chapters provide a detailed portrait of the Tea Party as faction. Each chapter teases out a theoretical expectation of a party, and evaluates its presence in the Tea Party using original data. I use a variety of statistical techniques to analzye these data, which I present using a combination of graphics and plain language explanations. Readers who are interested in additional information about these empirical analyses can consult the technical appendixes at the end of this book.

Chapter 2 develops this book's framework of factions in the United States. I explain what factions are, how they differ from other political subunits like social movements and interest groups, where they fit into party coalitions, and why some factions rely on insurgent strategies while others tend to cooperate.

Chapter 3 asks what would lead a faction to wage an insurgency against its own party. This chapter weaves together thirty-five in-depth interviews with Tea Party activists, uncovering their distrust of the Republican Party and their reasons for it. I supplement these interviews with findings on levels of trust in the Republican Party, taken from an original survey of Tea Party and Republican activists in Virginia, showing a marked difference between the views of Tea Partiers and those of other Republicans.

Chapter 4 investigates the strategy Tea Partiers used to generate electoral influence over the Republican Party in state and local elections across the country. Using an exhaustive list of local Tea Party groups that had an online presence between 2009 and 2015, I show that this insurgent faction mimicked the organizational structure of the party it sought to take over.

Chapter 5 describes the relationship between Tea Partiers' reactionary style of conservatism and their insurgent style of mobilization. I conduct a content analysis of Tea Party websites, blog posts, and interviews to draw out the status-threat dimension that undergirded the Tea Party's ideology.

Chapter 6 examines how an insurgent faction operates when in government (specifically Congress). Although Tea Party–affiliated candidates ran for office under the auspices of the Republican Party, they acted differently in Congress than did other Republicans. This chapter defines what it meant to be a Tea Partier in Congress, discussing the faction's development and growth through an analysis that compares the voting, cosponsorship, and press-release rhetoric of Tea Partiers with that of other Republicans.

Chapter 7 concludes by drawing out the ways an insurgent faction can destabilize and reconfigure its host party's coalition, with specific application to the 2016 Republican nomination of Donald Trump. I end with a discussion of the implications of the insurgent strategy for party politics writ large.

CHAPTER TWO

Miniature Parties within Parties

Factions are engines of political change that develop new ideas, refine them into workable policies, and promote them in government. — Daniel DiSalvo, *Engines of Change*[1]

"**P**arties and partisanship are indisputably the orphans of political philosophy," wrote Nancy Rosenblum.[2] Political philosophers are not alone in their disregard of parties. Even in its colloquial usage the word *partisan* is pejorative, typically referring to someone or something that is untowardly divisive. Despite their orphaned status, parties have come to enjoy a small cadre of champions in political science. As Schattschneider famously observed, ". . . Modern democracy is unthinkable save in terms of the political parties."[3]

To many, parties represent an example of Alexis de Tocqueville's lauded "secondary associations."[4] In contrast, factions are the Cinderella of political organizations, either forgotten or made to bear responsibility for any instability in parties. As a result, we lack the tools to explain intraparty conflicts with any degree of precision.

Understanding the different forms intraparty strife can take in the United States is especially important in the early twenty-first century, which has been marked by unprecedented levels of partisan divisiveness. Not only do the Democratic and Republican parties overlap with liberal and conservative ideologies in a more extreme way than ever before,[5] but the parties have also become increasingly polarized.[6] Scholarship documenting these trends tells us a lot about how the two parties differ from one another, but it does not reveal much about what goes on inside parties. In particular, we understand little about how parties' internal configurations—from policy priorities to dominant groups—change.

In this chapter I construct an architecture of subparty political groups that will allow us to explain how factions affect the dynamics within parties (and, by extension, the dynamics between parties). Factions, I contend, should be understood as miniature parties within party coalitions, through which groups of policy demanders can attempt to increase their influence in the party. I begin by reviewing what we know (and do not know) about factions in the United States. I then move to the foundational issue of where factions fit in party coalitions, after which I discuss how factions differ from other political groups like interest groups and social movements. Finally, I turn to the differences that can exist *between* factions, dividing them into two general types—consociational and insurgent—based on the strategies they use to challenge their host parties.

In the next several chapters, I use this architecture of factions to address some of the more confusing features of the Tea Party, including why it coopted the Republican Party's organizational apparatus, why its electoral strategy involved contesting Republican candidates, and why its demands extended beyond any one candidate or policy. Ultimately, this framework holds promise for illuminating factional episodes well beyond the first few decades of the twenty-first century. Until now, we have lacked a systematic way to explain surges of political energy, defaulting to the label of "movement." With the analytic tools to distinguish a faction from a movement, a faction from a policy-demanding group, and an insurgent faction from a more accommodating one, we can begin to understand why some groups trigger fundamental shifts in the party landscape, while others leave few traces.

Factions and Fractiousness

In an electoral landscape dominated by two major parties, factions rarely garner national attention. This shifted in 2015, when seventeen candidates announced that they would seek the 2016 Republican presidential nomination.[7] In an attempt to make sense of the crowded Republican primary field, journalists turned to the language of factions, understood as ideological "lanes." In one example, the *Washington Post* attempted to make sense of the crowded Republican primary field by dividing the Republican Party into five lanes (Tea Partiers, Evangelicals, moderate/establishment Republicans, very conservative Republicans, and libertarians) and describing the share of support each candidate could expect to receive from these factions.[8]

The "lanes" approach to factions raises more questions than it answers. Do parties always contain factions, or is this something new? Do factions correspond with different ideological approaches, and if so, how widespread are these ideological commitments among voters? Were factions to blame for crowded nomination fields, and if not, what is? In short: What are factions, and where do they fit into parties?

The answers to these questions are not readily available. Factions are a relatively new phenomenon, and the distinction between factions and parties is newer still. Indeed, the first extended discussions of factions in the sense of groups organized around political interests did not occur until the eighteenth century. In what is known as the Scottish Enlightenment, a generation of scholars pioneered the "scientific" study of politics. They built on the assumption that human behavior followed certain patterns throughout history, and that by studying how humans behaved in different societies, scholars could predict the outcomes of different political structures. One such pattern was the tendency of humans to divide into smaller groups based on personal interests, also known as factions.

Factions were of particular concern to David Hume, one of the most influential thinkers of the Scottish Enlightenment.[9] Hume was not particularly fond of factions. He saw them as instigators of conflict, as during the English Civil War of the mid-seventeenth century, in which members of two factions, the "court party" and the Puritans, "united themselves more intimately with their friends, and separated themselves wider from their antagonists."[10] Yet Hume was also convinced that factions were rooted in human nature, and would flourish the most in free societies like weeds in fertile soil. In other words, factions were a political inevitability, capable of both good and ill.[11]

Hume's views on factions became integral to the American experiment in 1787, via James Madison, a student of the Scottish school and fierce advocate of the proposed (but not yet ratified) US Constitution.[12] The new constitution had its critics, many of whom believed that the proposed federal government could not possibly be representative of or stably govern thirteen states that were spread out over such a large land mass. In response, Madison penned *Federalist* 10. Like Hume, he was wary of "the instability, injustice, and confusion" produced by factions, which he called "the mortal diseases under which popular governments have everywhere perished."[13] Similarly, Madison thought of factions as inevitable, explaining that the impulse to factionalize was "sown into the nature of man" and could not be eradicated without ridding humans of their liberty. Madison's enduring insight was not that factions were inevitable, but that they presented a solution to the representation problem. In such a large republic, he argued, factions representing multiple and diverse interests would proliferate. Competition between these factions would in turn produce a sort of self-enforcing equilibrium in which no one group would be able to achieve undue influence.

To Madison and Hume, factions and parties were the same thing: groups of like-minded individuals who organized to pursue a political interest. Indeed, until the Civil War the parties that emerged in the United States did not bear much semblance to modern parties in terms of organizational structures, voter bases, coalitions in government, and so forth.[14] As Austin Ranney explained in his 1975 book aptly titled *Curing the Mischiefs of Faction,* the United States had shifted from being a country in which parties *were* factions to being one in which two big-tent parties *contained* factions.[15] More recently, Daniel DiSalvo extended the Madisonian perspective to contemporary party factions. To DiSalvo, factions are "sown in the nature" of the US system and its two cumbersome big-tent parties. Not only are factions inevitable, but they also infuse parties with purpose, acting as "engines of political change that develop new ideas, refine them into workable policies, and promote them in government."[16]

Factions seem to be part and parcel of the US political system. This is not because of what Madison considered the human tendency to divide into groups, but it has something to do with the way the US parties developed. Of course factions, understood as groups pursuing particular political interests, exist in other political systems as well, but in a different form. In a multiparty electoral system, what we might call factions can more easily become minor parties. In a system that only allows for two major parties, factions manifest as miniature parties within a major party.

Building a Framework of Factions

The persistence of party factions does not mean, however, that all groups within a party are factions, that factions are the building blocks of parties, or even that all factions will use the same tactics. In what follows, I provide an architecture of factions. I begin by summarizing what factions are and where they fit in party coalitions. I then discuss how factions differ from other political groups in United States, such as interest groups and social movements. Finally, I explain how different strategies for achieving influence produce different types of factions.

US party factions cannot be understood apart from the peculiarities of the political system in which they develop, namely a two-party electoral system in two major coalition parties hold a monopoly on political influence. Factions represent the attempts of less influential political groups to elevate their status in their parties, and thus to increase their control over government and policy. In other words, factions are miniature parties within parties. To understand what it means to be a subparty, we need to understand a few basic features of contemporary US party coalitions.

Parties are what happens when a set of political actors turn an agreement to cooperate over time into a formal institution.[17] This arrangement, also known as a "long coalition," stems from the reality that a political actor will typically have a better chance of influencing policy by joining forces with others than by attempting to act alone. In contemporary US parties (i.e., since the McGovern-Fraser reforms of the 1970s), these political actors are often described as groups of policy demanders.[18] Although each of these policy-demanding groups has its own agenda, they compromise on a mutually acceptable slate of policies and candidates because each recognizes that its chances of influencing policy are greater if it cooperates than if it acts alone. Most of the time, most intraparty groups feel represented enough in their party's consensus that they agree to cooperate, and this results in relatively stable, faction-free party coalitions.[19]

That said, it is unlikely that a party's agenda will benefit all groups to the same extent. Those groups with the most influence in the party (whether due to size, resources, experience, or something else) will tend to benefit more, while groups with the least influence might not benefit at all. These low-influence groups not only have little incentive to compromise, but also lack the ability to increase their clout in the party on their own. These groups are the seeds of potential factions. In the event that multiple groups are left out of the party's consensus *and* these low-influence groups can agree to cooperate with one another, they could form a subcoalition (in the same way that groups form a party coalition in the first place). As a faction, these groups might have enough leverage to increase their influence in the party, and thus to gain control over the party's agenda.

The confluence of factors that give rise to a faction—a party agenda that excludes multiple low-influence groups, a calculation by influential groups in the party coalition that these low-influence groups do not present a credible threat, a set of excluded groups that have enough in common to form a subcoalition, and an agreement to form that subcoalition—is relatively rare. Yet these factors do occasionally converge, resulting in factions that, like the Tea Party, seek control over their party at any cost.

Distinguishing Factions from Interest Groups and Social Movements

Factions are often misdiagnosed as interest groups or social movements. Understanding the difference between factions and these other types of groups is important, because mistyping a group or failing to see its evolution from, say, movement to faction can blind us to both its strategy and its capacity for influence.

In a certain respect this is the story of the Tea Party, which was often referred to innocuously as the "Tea Party movement," when in reality grassroots mobilization and protest tactics were only integral to it in its earliest phase.[20] Some journalists, noting the disappearance of massive Tea Party protests on the national mall, erroneously claimed that it had disappeared. Others, confusing it with a movement, an interest group, or both, were at a loss to explain everything from the role of local Tea Party groups in David Brat's 2014 primary ousting of Republican incumbent Eric Cantor to how the Tea Party could possibly be connected to the rise of Donald Trump.[21] Rather than resulting in overly brittle boundaries, then, this method of differentiating political subtypes based on their relationship with a host party will allow us to better explain puzzling political episodes and where they fit in the larger political system.

Most basically, factions differ from other types of political entities—namely interest groups and movements—in their relationship to a host party. Although all three entities exist to pursue political outcomes broadly construed, factions are unique in two respects: they need a host party in order to exist, and they use the machinery of the host party to effect change. In contrast, interest groups and movements can and often do exist independently of a host party, and do not typically have direct access to a party's electoral machinery.

Interest groups and movements have their own trademark strategies and orbits of influence. Interest groups, for example, often engage in access-oriented behavior, in which they lobby both parties in an attempt to maximize access to policy influence.[22] This is to say not that interest groups cannot be members of party coalitions—many are policy-demanding groups within major parties—but simply that they need not be part of a party in order to be interest groups.[23]

Like interest groups, social and political movements need not work within a party to achieve their goals. Indeed, many of the most prominent US movements of the twentieth century represented groups that lacked access to traditional institutional channels. The signature features of movements—grassroots mobilization and the use of protests—were wrought of necessity.[24] Some see the hallmark of a successful social movement in its ability to gain access to traditional institutional channels by generating related interest groups or finding an ally in a major party. Yet a movement need not do so in order to exist; we need only think of movements like Occupy Wall Street, which refused association with either party (despite Democrats' best efforts).[25]

Of course, the boundaries that separate these subtypes from one another, much less from major parties, are often hazy at best.[26] Figure 2.1 depicts one possible configuration of these relationships. As a group within a party coalition that demands change from its host party, a faction necessarily exists within a party. That does not mean, how-

Relationship between sub-party organizations

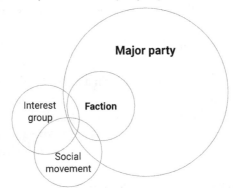

FIGURE 2.1. Factions are the only type of subparty group that exclusively mobilizes within a party.

ever, that what eventually becomes recognizable as a faction did not go through an earlier phase where it primarily used the protest tactics of a movement, something Heaney and Rojas describe as the "party in the street."[27] Similarly, movements may eventually spawn an infrastructure of interest groups, or even become absorbed by a party.[28] Finally, a faction may enjoy the support of aligned interest groups, as the Tea Party did with FreedomWorks and Americans for Prosperity.

Distinguishing Factions from One Another

Contemporary journalistic discussions often use "faction" to describe any visible manifestation of differences among co-partisans, from a presidential hopeful's supporters (e.g. a "Sanders faction"), to an ideological lane (e.g. "establishment conservatives").[29] More often than not, these apparent divisions are not factions at all, but the byproducts of routine negotiations within party coalitions over candidates and policy approaches. Indeed, these "factions" seem fundamentally different from a faction such as the Christian Right of the 1980s, which exerted significant influence on the policy goals and trajectory of its host party. To complicate matters further, even two factions that at first glance seem similar, such as the Christian Right and the Tea Party, can employ very different strategies and affect disparate outcomes.

How do we know what is and is not a faction, much less the impact a faction will have on its host party? In answer, I provide the final component of this framework of factions: a typology of factions based on the strategies they use to achieve influence. This typology centers on two questions, seen in figure 2.2. First, what does the faction demand from its host party? Second, what is the faction's strategy for enforcing its demands? The question of what a faction demands can be used to distinguish a "faction," in the sense of a routine division over a candidate or policy, from a miniature party within a party. I refer to groups that *only* demand something limited and specific, such as the nomination of a favored candidate, as particularistic factions. These are factions in the journalistic sense described previously; they crop up continuously within parties, especially in nomination contests and primaries. As part of the normal process by which a party negotiates its agenda, particularistic factions dissipate once their demand becomes irrelevant.

Not all factions demand something limited and specific, however.

Framework of faction types

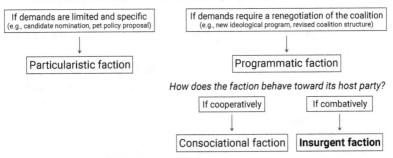

FIGURE 2.2. We can differentiate among faction types by examining how they behave towards their host parties.

Some factions' demands cannot be met short of a sweeping renegotiation of their coalition. We can call these factions *programmatic*. This kind of faction is a party within a party, developing a presence across various levels of party organization (local, state, national) in order to foment partywide change. Although a programmatic faction may issue specific demands or enthusiastically support a particular candidate, these demands are means to the end of taking over a party.

There is, however, more than one way of seeking partywide change. We can distinguish between programmatic factions by asking how they behave toward their host parties. Some programmatic factions establish cooperative power-sharing agreements with their host parties. We can think of these as *consociational* factions. Not all factions are able or willing to engage in such mutually beneficial arrangements. The second type of programmatic faction—an *insurgent* faction—is characterized by its combative posture toward its host party.

The Christian Right of the 1980s provides one of the most recent examples of a faction that primarily used a consociational strategy. It sought a renegotiation of the Republican Party's conservative consensus to prioritize religious traditionalism.[30] It asked the Republican Party to champion prayer in schools, pursue the reversal of *Roe v. Wade*, and protect traditional marriage. In return, the Christian Right offered a readily mobilized electoral base—something the Republican Party needed in order to regain its electoral footing after two decades of difficulties such as the insurgence of Goldwater conservatives, a party realignment, and the Watergate scandal.[31]

The Christian Right did use some insurgent tactics in its earlier days, such as targeting local conventions and contesting Republicans in primaries. But upon meeting with little resistance from the party establishment, the Christian Right entered into a consociational relationship with its host.[32] Why? Because both the Christian Right and the Republican Party stood to benefit from a power-sharing agreement.[33] A mere decade later, the faction was nearly indistinguishable from the Republican Party—not because the Christian Right had failed, but because it had successfully renegotiated the terms of the Republican coalition.

In contrast, an insurgent faction is marked by its willingness to use scorched-earth strategies if doing so will allow it to rule over the party's ashes. A faction might use insurgent strategies because it lacks sufficient leverage over the electorate to make a consociational arrangement attractive to its host party, or it may simply perceive the controlling interests in its host party as hostile to its demands. Whatever its reasons for mobilization, an insurgent faction is easily distinguished by the strategies it employs to force change.

The Tea Party is an example of such a faction, but it is not alone. Although they operated in a slightly different party era, the Southern Democrats (aka Dixiecrats) of 1932 to 1968 used insurgent strategies to increase their leverage within the Democratic Party. By the end of World War II, a fissure had emerged between the Democratic Party of the New Deal (and increasingly of civil rights), and the Democratic Party of the former Confederacy. In an attempt to reclaim their lost status in the Democratic Party, the Dixiecrats, in Congress and elsewhere, employed a growing number of insurgent tactics. In 1948 the Dixiecrats solidified their identity as a party faction, forming the States' Rights Democratic Party and running Strom Thurmond as a presidential candidate. Their initial goal was to capture the 127 electoral votes of the solid South to prevent either major party candidate from winning a majority, with the aim of throwing the election to the House of Representatives, where they hoped to gain concessions from other Democrats.[34]

Failing in their attempt at the presidency, Southern Democrats continued to pressure their party both in Congress and electorally. In Congress, they attempted to leverage the seats their caucus controlled in exchange for influence over the party's policy agenda and identity.[35] Regionally, they attempted to use the machinery of the existing Democratic Party to construct a platform for a separate party in the South.[36] In some states, such as Tennessee and Virginia, where Republicans occupied a strong enough position to pose an electoral threat, the Dixiecrats continued to work within the Democratic Party. In more solidly Democratic states, like Arkansas, they pursued a place on the ballot as a third party.[37]

The Dixiecrats overlapped to some extent with another example of an insurgent faction, this one in the Republican Party: the New Right that galvanized behind Barry Goldwater in 1964. Claiming to speak for McCarthyists, business owners, white Southerners, Catholics, Protestants, the working class, and anyone opposed to the New Deal, some in the New Right originally considered cooperating with Southern Democrats to nominate a traditionalist presidential candidate like George Wallace.[38] Later, key influencers in the faction—including radio host Clarence Manion, the *National Review*'s William F. Buckley, Phyllis Schafly, and the John Birch Society—galvanized in support of Senator Barry Goldwater as the 1964 Republican presidential nominee.[39]

Goldwater lost handily in the 1964 general election to Democratic incumbent Lyndon B. Johnson, but this did not dissuade the New Right from its attempts to gain influence in the Republican Party. Rather, this episode had taught them the power of using Republican Party's machinery against it. Leading up to 1964, the New Right had gained control of most of the Republican delegate base from areas of the Midwest, Southwest, and North. It had recruited key figures to deny delegates to the moderate Republican contender Nelson Rockefeller, inundated the press with messages about Goldwater's incumbent victory, and worked indirectly in local elections through a network of conservative activists.[40] Like the Dixiecrats, the Tea Party, and other insurgent factions, the New Right Republicans saw pressuring their host party to adopt a new conservative identity as being more important than short-term Republican electoral gains.

These two factions, the Dixiecrats and Goldwater's New Right, exerted deeply destabilizing influences over their host parties. They served as catalysts for the mid–twentieth century party realignment, solidified by the 1980s, in which the Republican Party became the home of conservatives of all stripes, from the small-government traditionalists who supported Goldwater to the white supremacists of the formerly solid Democratic South. In the following decades, the two parties increasingly aligned along a right-left ideological dimension, growing more polarized in the process.[41] Understood in this context, it is little wonder that the Tea Party has disrupted party business as usual. Its emergence in 2009 marks the first significant insurgent episode in more than four decades. The Tea Party pressured the Republican Party wherever it held power. In the midterm elections of 2010 and beyond, the Tea Party commandeered Republican machinery in local and state elections, national primaries, and eventually presidential nominations.

This brings us to the Tea Party. The Tea Party's willingness to undermine the Republican Party even at the risk of electoral losses to the opposing party baffled observers, who were accustomed to approaching electoral conflict in terms of Republicans opposing Democrats, not intraparty conflict. At first glance, the Tea Party did not seem to be at odds with its host party in any meaningful way. It proclaimed its desire for a smaller, more fiscally conservative government; so did the Republican Party. It chafed against Obama and other Democrats; so did the Republican Party.[42] Yet, as scholars began to investigate the views of Tea Party supporters, it became clear that something had been lost in translation. In their 2012 interviews with activists, Williamson and Skocpol were struck by an emphasis on immigration above and beyond emphases on traditional conservative issues.[43] Shortly thereafter, Parker and Barreto used data on Tea Party sympathizers in the mass public to argue that they were best described as *reactionary* conservatives. The Tea Party had much in common with previous groups that had reacted to a loss of racial and cultural dominance (including the Ku Klux Klan, and others who resisted civil rights) and to a lost way of life (such as the John Birch Society and the America Firsters, who were among Goldwater's supporters).

The account of the Tea Party that I present here is consistent with that of Parker and Barreto, but it goes one step further. I suggest that it is no coincidence that two of the most striking earlier incidents of insurgent factions (e.g. the Dixiecrats and Goldwater's New Right) combined a reactionary style of mobilization with a reactionary ideology. Similarly, viewing the Tea Party's reactionary ideology in the context of its mobilization as an insurgent faction—in itself a reaction to the established Republican Party coalition—provides a clearer understanding not only of the Tea Party's impact on the Republican Party, but also of its place in US history.

The following chapters investigate different aspects of what it means to view the Tea Party as an insurgent faction. I combine Tea Party activists' own descriptions of their motives and strategy with observational measures of the Tea Party's behavior. In this way, I intend to probe the nature of the Tea Party's disagreement with its host party, of its organizational apparatus and connection to elites, of the political and organizational outcomes of its reactionary ideology, of the development and issue priorities of its members in Congress, and, finally, of Donald Trump as the heir of its insurgency.

In particular, I argue that the Tea Party's expression of reactionary conservatism had two key expressions: one ideological, and one institutional. Ideologically, the Tea Party contested the Republican Party in an attempt to prioritize protection of the American national identity from any perceived threat—from liberals, the government, Republicans, immigrants, refugees, or terrorists—over the economic or social conservatism of decades past. Institutionally, the Tea Party represented the apex of a long distrust of elites and political insiders. It often expressed this distrust in the language of government accountability, but this had to do less with maintaining a limited federal government than with the destruction of established figures in both parties, institutional norms, and even the Tea Party's connection to inside-the-Beltway groups like FreedomWorks and Americans for Prosperity. It is to this distrust of the Republican Party that we now turn.

CHAPTER THREE

What's Wrong on the Right?
Why the Tea Party Contested
the Republican Party

When you pinpoint that the Republican Party is just as corrupt as any other party, it's blinding, it's like you hit them between the eyes because no one has ever confronted them with the truth. . . . The future of the Tea Party will involve a very bloody fight with the Republican Party. — Bob Shannon, local Tea Party leader, in an interview in March 16, 2012

In 2009, the Tea Party was mostly a mood. Its protests provided an outlet for conservatives who were distressed by the failing economy and Republican losses in the 2008 election. As the 2010 midterm elections approached, many Republicans used the Tea Party as a rallying cry to encourage conservatives to turn out and vote.[1] None of this was particularly unusual; the Tea Party was certainly not the first partisan group to protest a new president, or to stage a comeback in the midterm elections following major electoral losses.[2] But as the dust settled and Republicans began to focus on the 2010 midterms, it became increasingly clear that the Tea Party represented a shift from partisan politics as usual. It was no friend of the left, but it was becoming an unreliable ally for the Republican Party as well.

The Tea Party's rift with its host party was perplexing, especially given an apparent lack of conflict between the Tea Party's vocal commitment to fiscal conservatism and that of the Republican Party.[3] What exactly was the nature of the Tea Party's ill will toward its host?

The answer is not particularly straightforward. Much of the Tea Party's opposition to the Republican Party came from activist-run local

Tea Party groups, and activists are notoriously difficult to track down. Some political scientists skirted this issue by analyzing public opinion surveys, but these were ill-suited to the study of subpopulations such as Tea Party activists. The likelihood of even a few Tea Party activists being in a survey sample was so low that researchers tended to rely on the responses of people who said they *sympathized* with the Tea Party. Given that most Republicans were sympathetic to the Tea Party in its heyday, from around 2010 to 2014, this approach did not yield much information about the Tea Party activists who formed the faction's core, or why they sought to undermine their own party.[4]

To solve this problem, I went directly to Tea Party activists, attending countless group meetings, protests, and training sessions. Through these repeated interactions I built a rapport with several leaders of local groups, many of whom agreed to interviews and put me in contact with other activists in their groups. Between 2012 and 2014, I conducted a total of thirty-five in-depth interviews with Tea Party activists from ten states: Alabama, Colorado, Georgia, Mississippi, New York, Pennsylvania, Tennessee, Virginia, Utah, and Washington. In addition to these interviews, I was able to obtain a list of delegates to the 2013 nominating convention of the Republican Party of Virginia (RPV). Nominating conventions are thought to contain the "fullest representation of the party activist corp at any given moment," and delegate lists to these conventions provide a rare opportunity to survey party activists.[5] Immediately following Virginia's statewide elections in November 2013, I fielded the Virginia Politics Study (VPS), a survey of the RPV delegates. The responses of 1,600 state Republican delegates (one-third of whom were Tea Partiers, two-thirds of whom were not) provides a unique opportunity to compare the views of Tea Partiers and establishment Republicans side by side.[6]

Taken together, the interviews and the survey produce a rare glimpse at the motivations of Tea Party activists. In keeping with popular perceptions of the early Tea Party, the activists initially mobilized in reaction to the many changes facing Americans in 2009. As they gained their political footing, they began to question the Republican Party's commitment to "conservative" principles. They did not take issue with the party's policy stances per se; they tended to agree with establishment or non–Tea Party Republicans on the importance of reducing government spending, defending traditional marriage, stemming the flow of immigrants, and maintaining a strong military. For Tea Party activists, adherance to conservative principles meant a general resistance to change. In the absence of a credible commitment from their host party, they sought to hold the party accountable by offering Republicans a choice: adopt the Tea Party's style of conservatism or else face an electoral challenge from the right.

The Perfect Storm: Activists' Initial Motivations

When asked what initially led them to join the Tea Party, many activists pointed to the events of late 2008 and early 2009, including the economic crash, the "big government's" corporate bailouts, Obama's election, and the passage of Obamacare. They described these events as a "perfect storm," a "breaking point," a "tipping point," and a "reawakening." Susan,*[7] a former animal rights activist and Ross Perot supporter, explained, "A lot of stuff happened all at once. George Bush at the end, then Obamacare, and all the big spending, and it all happened at once in one big explosion. I think that's what woke people up." For the "first time in my life," she explained, bursting into tears, "I really feel scared for my country." Paul T., former leader of the Mississippi Tea Party, described the events as a "perfect storm" that woke up conservatives who were "pulling themselves up by their bootstraps," and alerted them to the "socialism" coming out of the Obama campaign. Mary* argued, "There's been a bit of a reawakening. Something changed in the moral fiber of the country very distinctly with Obamacare."

A Colorado Tea Party leader, Regina T., called the bailouts "the genesis and Obamacare the match that caused things to explode." She thought this combination fueled the Tea Party, producing "raw passion from everyday people who are scared about the country." Gary,* a Tea Party activist from southwest Virginia, said he had joined the Tea Party because all the events of 2008 and 2009 had made him "mad" and "fed up with anti-America, anti-capitalism, and anti-God." Meredith* communicated these sentiments in milder language: "For me it was a cumulative thing. All of those things impacted me and reminded me that things weren't going in the right direction."

Some Tea Partiers singled out the person of Barack Obama as their catalyst for mobilization. In a surprisingly impassioned outburst, Mary, an otherwise soft-spoken woman, declared:

Without a doubt, this whole Obama administration has made me ashamed to be an American. I cannot believe that he is trampling and trashing on our constitution everyday. Not just him, but his cohort also. They are blatant and brazen about it. When he says, "I don't care what Congress says, I'll just get around them," are you kidding me? You don't have that power. Not by the same document I've read.

Brian S., a lawyer and activist in Bucks County, Pennsylvania, also attributed his involvement to Obama's election:

I joined the Tea Party because I was in shock when Obama was elected. He wouldn't wear the flag on his lapel, and hated white people. He was different even than Clinton, who cooperated with Newt. Obama is a phony. He got rid of Churchill's bust in the White House, his father was part of a colonialist antiwhite group in Africa, and his mother was a raging leftist. Obama's real agenda was destructive. He meant to dismantle the country.

Sandy,* a stay-at-home mom from Alabama who had traveled to DC to attend an "impeach Obama" rally, put it this way: "I want the country back the way it was, and I don't think Obama wants the same thing." At the same rally, seventy-seven-year-old Patti* explained that she had joined the Tea Party because "Obama and the IRS are going to become like the Nazi German police force." Jim Bacon, a conservative Virginia activist and blogger who worked closely with the Tea Party, put these various comments in context. In his estimation, it was "the activist, statist agenda of the Obama administration that got things going." Only later had the Tea Party begun to examine the "complexities of the constitution and fiscal policy."

Not all Tea Partiers had such a visceral reaction to Obama, however. Many of the Tea Party's early leaders, especially those tied to its umbrella organizations, were initially drawn to it because of its potential as a vehicle for fiscally libertarian principles. As Matt Kibbe, president and CEO of FreedomWorks, explained: "It started with anger about TARP [a government program to address foreclosures in the wake of the 2008 economic crisis], and frankly the values underlying that fight were that you should treat everyone like everybody else." Mark Daugherty, part of the VATPPF leadership committee, explained that the collapse of the financial markets between fall 2008 and March 2009 had created "a lot of fear about loss of personal wealth that coincided with a big deficit. The bail-out program alienated a lot of the Tea Party folks." The national debt, which had increased under Bush and showed no sign of stopping under Obama, resulted in a "snowball effect that concerned folks enough to get involved. Americans to some degree suffer from inertia in their individual lives with families and work, but things reached a flashpoint in early 2009." Matt P., a filmaker and activist from New York City, said he had identified as a liberal until December 2008, when Bush launched a $168 billion economic stimulus package in response to the economic downturn. To Matt P., this stimulus package seemed "socialistic." He began to seek answers from free-market advocates like Glenn Beck and Thomas Sowell, an effort that led him to libertarianism and the Tea Party.

Although economics was cited as an impetus for Tea Party mobilization most frequently by the more nationally focused leaders and activists, some local activists pointed to it as well. For example, Anastasia Pryzbylski had grown concerned during the 2008 election cycle when reading Peter Shift's book *Up and Coming Economic Collapse*, after which she began to see signs of economic collapse in America. She recalled being "upset with [2008 Republican presidential nominee] McCain's response, especially about mortgages," but had seen Obama as "the greater of the two evils because he seemed more radical." Her alarm grew when, shortly after taking office, Obama pumped more federal money into the economy and gave a "centrist"-sounding State of the Union address. In response, Pryzbylski became part of the early Tea Party efforts in Bucks County, Pennsylvania, and she eventually led her own Tea Party group, the Kitchen Table Patriots.

A final set of activists attributed their initial involvement in the Tea Party to the passage of Obamacare in 2009. Mike* described Obamacare as a "socialist" policy, a term that frightened him. To Mary, Obamacare was "absolutely the nail in the coffin for me. That was so absolutely unconstitutional and against the wish of the people. That was my turning point." Martin* agreed, calling health care "the catalyst in terms of getting involved." It was so serious to him that it was not even "a party thing." Paul T. explained that, for him and some of the other small business owners in his Mississippi community, the combination of Rick Santelli's 2009 televised "rant" calling for the formation of a Tea Party and the debate about Obamacare had "lit the fuse." They had realized that, "if Obamacare went through, the cost added to each of us would mean it would become increasingly hard to survive as small business owners."

Yvonne Donnelly, Glenn Beck's sister-in-law and a coordinator for the Glenn Beck's 9/12 Group umbrella organization,[8] recalled her "tipping point" as having occurred in early 2009. It had begun with the bailouts under Bush, she said, and "snowballed from there. Health care was potentially the bigger issue. People were saying, 'Wait, this isn't right.'" She felt that "the pedal had been pushed all the way to the floor in the fundamental transformation of America. People were being told they were going to fundamentally change America and the concept America was founded on."

The Layers of the Tea Party's Distrust of the GOP

When explaining their distrust of the Republican Party, activists often established a dichotomy between "real" conservatives like themselves, and the RINOs who were responsible for the party's drift from conservatism. In the words of Jenny Beth Martin, leader of the Tea Party Patriots umbrella organization, the Tea Party was "not an inside, but an outside force. . . . We deliberately did not try to go into and live in DC and become another DC organization. We were trying to do things differently because of the way things had happened in our country, and how both parties had done things wrong, and wanted it outside of the party system." Later, she referred to the Republican and Democratic parties alike as the "opposition" because they did not share the goals of "normal, average Americans."

Some people's distrust of elites ran so deep that they discriminated between real Tea Party groups like their own and the large national Tea Party organizations, which they saw as mouthpieces of the Republican Party. The Tea Party Express, Americans for Prosperity, and Freedom-Works were most frequently on the receiving end of these attacks, thanks to their ties to establishment donors like the Koch brothers and their use of DC offices. John G., who at one point led the Northern Virginia Tea Party, put it this way: "The Tea Party Express was mostly run by Republican hacks. Very few groups had any sort of grassroots involvement that was meaningful. Mostly they are the typical inside-the-beltway operators." Paul T. expressed similar sentiments, explaining that the "main Tea Party" had done more damage to the cause than anything else. So much so, in fact, that the Mississippi Tea Party groups (including the one he led) refused to accept grants from FreedomWorks, focusing instead on building a network of grassroots Mississippi organizations with the help of other local activists.

On the surface, Tea Partiers were fundamentally suspicious of establishment Republicans because they were "elites." Yet the rift between the Tea Party and the Republican Party was more complex than a populist conflict between the people and the elites; this was only the first layer. Tea Partiers made it clear that their real issue with Republican insiders was their lack of accountability to conservative principles. In other words, the term "elite" was code for "not accountable to people like us." The second layer involved a solution: pressuring the Republican Party to adhere to Tea Party principles.

What were these principles? Although Tea Partiers emphasized fiscal conservatism, they did not actually register any disagreements with the Republican Party on policy content. The main difference between Tea Party activists and their establishment counterparts, at least in the delegate survey, was one of intensity. This is because, as I discuss in more detail in chapter 5, Tea Partiers' conservatism was about resistance to change, not adherance to a policy program.

Keeping Republicans Accountable

To Mike, the difference between the Tea Party and its host was simple: "The Republican Party's all about getting elected, period," while the Tea Party was "about principle." A Tea Party member, he said, should not "elect someone because they have an *R* behind their name. I believe in three things: limited government, fiscal reform, and free markets, period. If you stand for those three things, even if you tell me you're a communist, I'll vote for you!" Mary underscored the importance of what she called the United States' "founding" principles of "fiscal responsibility and liberty." If a candidate believed in these "founding" principles, "I would vote either way and have no problem, and mean it truly." Otherwise, her main goal was to make "the people doing this accountable, and I'm deadly serious about this." Bob S., a Tea Party leader in southern Virginia, explained the Tea Party's issue with the Republican Party in visceral terms:

> When you pinpoint that the Republican Party is just as corrupt as any other party, it's blinding, it's like you hit them between the eyes because no one has ever confronted them with the truth. . . . The future of the Tea Party involves a very bloody fight with the Republican Party.

This theme of accountability undergirded the Tea Party's electoral strategy: replacing corrupt Republicans with Tea Partiers, and making sure that the new officeholders remained true to the Tea Party's ideals (although what these ideals were was somewhat unclear, as we will see later in this chapter). This is perhaps best summed up in Regina T's view of what success would look like for the Tea Party: "We would gradually elect more people who understand the Constitution, not those driven by avarice, wealth, power, or influence. If you get enough people like this in office, we won't have to scream so loud."

As succinctly explained by John G., a cofounder of the VATPPF, the Tea Partiers' goal was that of "making the GOP hurt" in elections. Across the board, local leaders explained that their groups were doing whatever was necessary to gain a seat at the table. For example, Tea Partiers in areas with strong Republican Party organizations operated by infiltrating the party. Mark Daugherty observed that a "healthy portion" of Tea Party members participated in local Republican party meetings in order to "remind the Republican party of the creed of individual responsibility." In particular, members often participated in the local Republican Party so that they could "have a voice at the convention in terms of selection of candidates." In many of the more rural areas, Tea Party members did not associate with the Republican Party at all, but worked with "Tea Party candidates" because more "congruence" existed between these candidates and Tea Party principles than between establishment Republican Party candidates and the Tea Party.

Tea Partiers were quick to note that working through the GOP did not mean a compromise with the party. In Pennsylvania, Brian S. explained, the Tea Party was working through the Republican Party because "the Tea Party is being pragmatic. Parties are machines. The machine in the GOP is willing to take the Tea Party's help." Jim Bacon explained how crucial it was to the Republican Party that "the Tea Party is not a branch of the GOP, but exercises influence on the GOP," and that if "any other group could act as a viable player in the political marketplace, the Tea Party might drop their support for the Republican Party."

To contextualize the difference between Tea Partiers' views of the Republican Party and those of other Republican activists, we can look to the opinions of delegates to the 2013 RPV nominating convention. As might be expected, Tea Partiers demonstrated stronger anti-Democratic and anti-Obama sentiments than establishment Republicans did. More striking, however, was the heightened distrust of the Republican Party expressed by Tea Partiers across multiple questions.

The first of these questions gave respondents a series of statements describing how some people felt during 2008 and 2009, when the financial crisis began and Barack Obama was elected president. Respondents were asked to select whatever options corresponded with what they remembered feeling at the time. The options included "distrust of both parties," "distrust of Congress," "anger at Bush," "anger at Wall Street," "anger at mortgage defaulters," "anger at Obama," "scared of socialism," "scared about the US's financial future," and "scared about my personal financial future."

Figure 3.1 shows differences in how Tea Partiers and establishment Republicans responded to this question. Each of the bars corresponds with the proportion of respondents in that group who indicated that they remembered experiencing that feeling in 2008 and 2009. Tea Party responses are indicated here and elsewhere by darker-colored bars, and

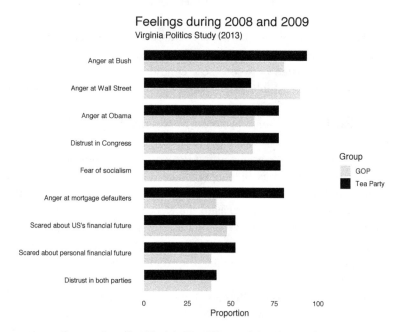

FIGURE 3.1. Compared to other Virginia Republican activists, Tea Partiers were more distrustful of President George W. Bush, Congress, and both parties.

establishment Republicans are referred to as "GOP." Tea Partiers and establishment Republican were equally likely to say they had been angry at Wall Street (51 percent of establishment Republicans and 48 percent of Tea Partiers), angry at mortgage defaulters (39 percent of establishment Republicans and 42 percent of Tea Partiers), scared about the financial future of the United States (78 percent of establishment Republicans and 79 percent of Tea Partiers), and scared about their personal financial futures (both at 53 percent).

But there were a few options that distinguished Tea Partiers from their Republican counterparts. Two of these are not particularly surprising, given what we know about the Tea Party. Eighty-one percent of Tea Partiers were afraid of socialism, as opposed to 62 percent of establishment Republicans. When it came to anger at Obama, 94 percent of Tea Partiers chose this option, as opposed to 78 percent of establishment Republicans. It is the remaining three response options, all of which involve distrust and/or Republicans, that most distinguish Tea Partiers from their establishment counterparts. Sixty-three percent of Tea Partiers reported feeling distrust toward both parties, as opposed to only 39 percent of establishment Republicans. Although neither group harbored particularly warm sentiments toward Congress, 90 percent of Tea Partiers registered distrust of that body, as opposed to 81 percent of establishment Republicans. Finally, Tea Partiers noted anger at the most recent Republican president, George W. Bush, at 64 percent, as opposed to 42 percent of establishment Republicans.

It is likely, given the gap between 2008 and the fielding of this survey in 2013, that answers to this question had more to do with respondents' current feelings about politics than with their past feelings. Regardless, the results convey important information about Tea Partiers' heightened distrust of the Republican Party. Tea Partiers remembered feeling greater animus toward Obama and clearer fear of socialism, but their anger at the sitting Republican president and distrust of both parties presents the most substantial difference between their attitudes and those of establishment Republicans.

The survey includes two other questions that can help us understand the nature of Tea Partiers' distrust of the Republican Party. The first asked respondents about their level of trust in the most recent Republican presidential candidate, Mitt Romney. The second asked them to indicate their favorability toward a wider array of political actors, including some Tea Party favorites.

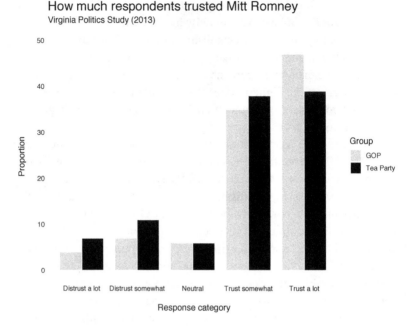

How much respondents trusted Mitt Romney
Virginia Politics Study (2013)

FIGURE 3.2. Compared to other Virginia Republican activists, Tea Partiers were less trusting of 2012 Republican presidential nominee Mitt Romney.

Respondents received the following question in regard to Mitt Romney: "Thinking back again to the 2012 presidential election, when Mitt Romney was the Republican nominee, how much did you trust Mitt Romney to lead the country?" Options ranged from 1 ("distrust a lot") to 5 ("trust a lot"). The distribution of responses for Tea Party and establishment Republicans can be seen in figure 3.2. The most common responses across groups were "trust somewhat" and "trust a lot." This is not necessarily surprising, given that the survey sample was made up of Virginia Republican delegates. That said, Tea Partiers were somewhat less likely to say that they trusted Romney "a lot," and more likely to say that they distrusted him "a lot" or "somewhat."

These results are consistent with the story of distrust from the interviews, but not by a large margin. It is possible, of course, that when asked about Romney alone, respondents associated his name with that of his opponent, Barack Obama, whom both Tea Partiers and establishment Republicans had opposed. The second question about political figures provides insights into the distinctions Tea Partiers drew among Republicans. Respondents were asked to indicate their favorability toward a variety of political figures (and one organization, the US Chamber of Commerce).

A little over half of these political figures were nonestablishment individuals who were associated in some way with the Tea Party. These included libertarian Senator Ron Paul, Tea Party darlings Senator Ted Cruz and former vice-presidential candidate Sarah Palin, the conservative Virginia lieutenant governor candidate E. W. Jackson, the conservative Republican Virginia gubernatorial candidate Ken Cuccinelli, and the Christian-Right activist Michael Farris. The other four were establishment Republican figures, namely Virginia Senator George Allen, Virginia Governor Bob McDonnell, Republican House Speaker John Boehner, and the US Chamber of Commerce. If distrust—or, at the very least, poor opinions—of the Republican Party distinguished Tea Partiers from other Republicans, then we would expect them to approve more strongly of nonestablishment figures, and less strongly of establishment figures. Figure 3.3 shows the average ranking each group of

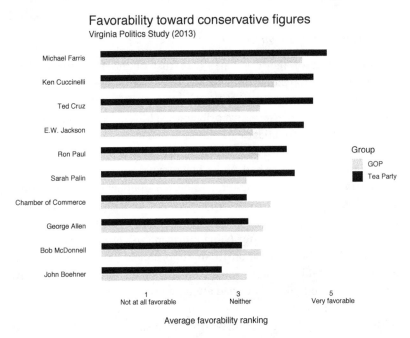

FIGURE 3.3. Tea Partiers favored nonestablishment conservatives.

respondents (Tea Partiers and establishment Republicans) gave that political figure on a one-to-five favorability scale, going from not at all favorable (1) to very favorable (5).

Tea Partiers and establishment Republicans only concurred on two
figures. Michael Farris, a Virginia Christian Right activist, received the
highest average favorability ranking from both groups. Ken Cuccinelli,
that year's Republican gubernatorial candidate, received the second
highest average favorability ranking from both groups. Notably, Tea Partiers were more enthusiastic in their rankings of these two candidates,
with higher mean scores. The remainder of the results are in line with
what we might expect. Tea Partiers were substantially more favorable toward Ted Cruz, E. W. Jackson, Ron Paul, and Sarah Palin. In contrast,
establishment Republicans, though tepid toward everyone, gave higher
average rankings to the US Chamber of Commerce (their next favorite after Cuccinelli), George Allen, Bob McDonnell, and John Boehner
than Tea Partiers did. In short, these results mark a division between
Tea Partiers and establishment Republicans, with Tea Partiers showing high levels of favorability toward nonestablishment Republicans, in
keeping with the strategies we would expect from an insurgent faction.

Insufficient Commitment to Conservatism

Although some of the Tea Party's distrust of the Republican Party
seemed to be a reflection on *who* was in charge, some of it had to do
with the Tea Party's perception that the Republican Party could not be
trusted to fight for conservative principles. The Tea Party thus saw it as
their job to hold Republicans accountable.

As Shaun* summarized, "We have an issue with Republicans on
big spending, just not as bad as the Democrats, not as big." Most of the
Tea Party activists I interviewed had been Republicans for some time,
but had grown frustrated with what they saw as the party's lack of re-
sponsiveness. Donna* had been a registered Republican since 1982, but
turned to the Tea Party after being "thrown out" of her local Republican Party over her opposition to an "unprincipled candidate." Tricia*
and her husband had always voted Republican, but became more active
when they retired. First they tried attending Republican Party meetings,
but thought the party was "so weak that we weren't learning or accom-
plishing anything." One day, they drove by a sign advertising Tea Party
meetings. They went to the next one, and finally felt that they had found

others who "believe[d] in freedom" and were focused on "real change." Brian S. had attended Republican Party meetings and fundraisers in the past, but had become "nauseated by the GOP and its liking for big government." After moving to Colorado in 2007, Regina T. received Glenn Beck's e-newsletter and saw a link about a need for grassroots precinct leaders to take over the Colorado Republican Party. She attended two caucus trainings and tried to get involved with her local party organization, but the county leader was unresponsive and disinterested.

To Regina, this episode exemplified the failings of the contemporary Republican Party: Republican officeholders were only "interested in the title" and not "invested in the process or in finding good candidates." As Paul T. stated, "The GOP has drifted from principles, and there isn't a lot of difference between the two major parties in Washington. The GOP says smaller government, but whenever they get their hands on the government it doesn't get any smaller. They want to direct how it's going to grow." In Donna's words, both parties were in "loyal opposition" and simply wanted big government, whereas the Tea Party wanted "self-government under the people."

In general, Tea Partiers saw a disconnect between their idea of conservatism and that of the Republican Party. The VPS included a pair of questions that allow us to get at this more systematically. Delegates to the RPV nominating convention were asked whether they saw themselves as more conservative, about the same, or less conservative than the Republican Party in Congress. The same question was asked about the Republican Party in Virginia.[9] Importantly, I did not define conservatism for respondents, thus allowing the answers to reflect respondents' personal evaluations of what conservatism meant for them, and whether they felt their ideals were represented by the Republican Party.

Figure 3.4 shows these rankings. The set of bars on the left corresponds with answers to the question about the Republican Party in Congress, and the set of bars on the right corresponds with answers to the question about the Republican Party in Virginia. The first bar in both sets shows the percentage of establishment Republican delegates who chose each response option, and the second bar shows the responses of Tea Party delegates.

Two patterns emerge from these results. First, Tea Partiers viewed themselves as being uniformly more conservative than the Republican Party. They were nearly twice as likely as establishment Republicans to evaluate themselves as more conservative than Republicans in

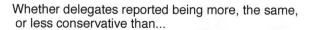

Whether delegates reported being more, the same, or less conservative than...

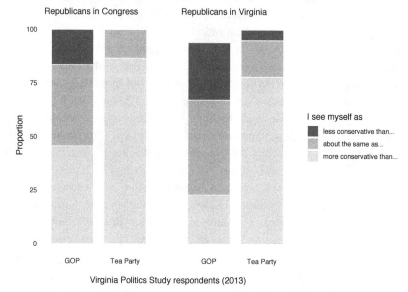

FIGURE 3.4. Tea Party activists saw themselves as more conservative than the Republican Party, both in Congress and in their states. This was not the case for non–Tea Party Republican activists.

Congress (86 percent versus 45.6 percent). Second, despite being delegates to the Virginia Republican nominating convention, the Tea Partiers did not see themselves as being in line with the Virginia Republican Party. They were over three times more likely than establishment respondents to see themselves as more conservative than Republicans in Virginia (77.9 percent versus 22.9 percent). In short, the Tea Partiers perceived a sizable ideological divide between themselves and the Republican Party, especially when asked about the state in which they were waging their insurgency.

A final question remains: Were there certain policy issues on which Tea Partiers saw themselves as more conservative than the Republican Party, or was this difference one of intensity? To assess this, we can turn to a survey question that asked respondents to prioritize a variety of issues. Respondents were given a list of contemporary policy issues, including cutting taxes, reducing the size of government, cutting the national debt, repealing Obamacare, putting a stop to illegal immigration,

decreasing the number of abortions, defining marriage as being between one man and one woman, putting prayer back in schools, protecting the United States from terrorism, and electing Republicans. They
were asked to rank the importance of these issues on a one-to-five scale,
from "not at all important" to "very important." Figure 3.5 shows the
percentage of Tea Partiers and establishment Republicans in the sample who chose option 5 ("very important") for each of the policy issues
in question.

Based on these results, Tea Partiers and establishment Republicans
did not possess wildly different opinions on policy ends. The real difference lay in the greater propensity of Tea Partiers to rank nearly every
issue as "very important," including economics, repealing Obamacare,
putting a stop to illegal immigration, reducing the number of abortions, defining marriage as between one man and one woman, and putting prayer back in schools. The only exceptions were protecting America from terrorism, reducing unemployment, and electing Republican

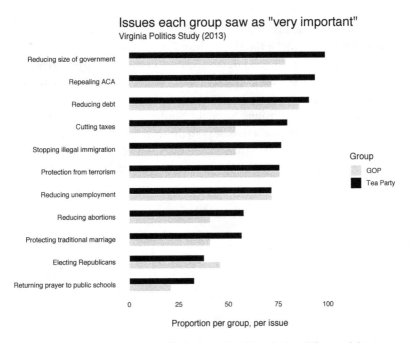

FIGURE 3.5. Tea Partiers were more likely than other Virginia Republican activists to see
multiple policy issues as "very important."

candidates. The key difference between Tea Partiers and establishment Republicans on policy issues was one of intensity—Tea Partiers felt more strongly about nearly every issue. As I demonstrate in chapter 5, this is because the Tea Party's vision of conservatism had much more to do with resistance to change than with any policy program.

Summary: Why the Tea Party Turned on Its Host

Unlike other conservative activists, Tea Partiers saw the Republican Party as fundamentally untrustworthy. They felt that the Republican Party had perpetrated a massive bait-and-switch: using the rhetoric of conservatism, but doing little to stop their country's steady march away from conservative principles. In their interviews they described this shift as both personally upsetting (in terms such as "afraid," "scared for," "mad," "fed up," "ashamed," "suspicious," "meltdown") and disastrous for the country as a whole (using words like "socialism," "perfect storm," "breaking," "tipping," "explosion," "change," "destruction," "statism," "Nazism," "snowball effect," "flashpoint," "centrism"). Things were happening that alarmed them, and they felt powerless. In response, the Tea Partiers sought to make the Republican Party "hurt."

In the next two chapters I detail the ways in which the Tea Party organized against the Republican Party, and the content of Tea Party–style conservatism. In chapter 4 I trace the extensive organizational network that local Tea Party groups formed in order to wage their insurgency, and I explain why this rebellion was so difficult for the Republican Party to quash. In chapter 5 I return to the question of the Tea Party's conservative principles, explaining the reactive nature of the Tea Party's insurgency.

CHAPTER FOUR

Mobilizing the Insurgency: The Tea Party's Federated Organization

The Tea Party has no leader. It has no address, no phone and no Washington headquarters. It is everywhere and nowhere. — Richard Cohen (journalist), 2010[1]

I first began researching the Tea Party when I lived in Washington, DC. The nation's capital attracts people who want to influence politics and policy, and who see working through the US federal government as the most straightforward way to do so. This assumption was reflected in how most Washingtonians reacted when they heard I was writing on the Tea Party. "The Tea Party—aren't they kind of disorganized? They don't really have a leader or anything. How do they expect to achieve anything?"

The equivocation between organization and central leadership was not confined to these casual encounters. Spectators often cited the Tea Party's lack of leadership when explaining that it was not a cause for concern, could not change anything, and would soon disappear. It was this false equivalency between leadership and organization that blinded many to the Tea Party's chief means of achieving influence: mimicking the structure of its host party, especially at the state and local level. Local Tea Party leaders, frequently veterans of local Republican politics, seemed to understand the federated structure of US parties better than their nationally focused commentators did. In order to win key national positions, Tea Party activists repeatedly explained, they first had to gain control of the Republican Party's electoral apparatus at the state and local levels.

This chapter provides a comprehensive overview of the network through which the Tea Party achieved its influence. By combining a unique data set of local Tea Party websites and blogs with social network analysis techniques, I detail the structure of the Tea Party, including the places where groups were most likely to mobilize, and the elites to which they looked for information.

Like those of many insurgencies, the Tea Party's structure reflected that of its host,[2] which in this case was the federated structure of a major US political party. This included a cadre of elite Tea Party voices, many of whom were conservative media figures. These figures led the Tea Party much as national party organizations also lead their parties, setting the tone for conversations on national issues and distributing additional money and resources to candidates. Most of the local groups' action, however, was clustered regionally. The Tea Party's larger battle with the Republican Party is, I argue, best understood as the sum of myriad smaller insurgencies through which it systematically gained influence over the Republican Party from the ground up.

What It Means to View the Tea Party as a Network

Eric Cantor became the US House representative for Virginia's 7th congressional district in 2000. His district was solidly Republican, and Cantor was a rising star in the party. He was on a list of potential running mates for presidential candidate John McCain in 2008, and he became House majority leader in 2011. At the beginning of 2014, there was little question that Cantor would once again win handily and maintain his place in House leadership. But he did not even make it to the general election. In May 2014 he faced a primary challenge from political newcomer David Brat. Brat's candidacy did not attract much attention from the national Republican Party or the DC-based Tea Party political action committees (PACs)—that is, until he beat Cantor by a margin of nearly 11 percent in the district's Republican primary.[3]

Brat, it turns out, had received substantial support from the Tea Party all along—just not from national Tea Party PACs. Virginia's 7th congressional district was home or adjacent to multiple local Tea Party groups. These groups considered Cantor a "RINO," and had been targeting him for some time. Indeed, Brat was not even the first Tea Party candidate who had primaried Cantor; the Tea Party-identifying Floyd Bayne had vied for Cantor's seat in 2012. Having learned from their primary loss in 2012, the Tea Parties in Virginia's 7th were more organized in 2014.

Their coordination efforts were public and obvious, occurring via their web pages and social networking sites.[4]

Still, this was only one primary in one congressional district in one state. Did the Tea Party organize in similar ways elsewhere, and to what extent? To answer these questions, I turned to the Tea Party's unique and highly visible use of websites for organization and information dissemination. In the Tea Party's most active period (2010–14), nearly every local group had an active website, blog, or social media page (information about website list creation and data collection can be found in the appendix to this chapter). Lacking the infrastructure of major parties, local Tea Party groups relied on these websites to communicate information to their members. Every website gave an address for a group's meeting place, and I used these to geocode the groups on the basis of their zip codes. Most of the websites also contained one or more of these additional pieces of information: mission statements, blog posts by group leaders, and links to external websites.

This chapter focuses on two questions: With whom were Tea Party groups connected, and where did they mobilize? To answer the first question, I created a network of connections between local Tea Party groups and outside organizations using the links on Tea Partiers' websites.[5] This network allows us to answer several questions about the Tea Party's organization, including where groups clustered, to whom or what they looked for information, and how they connected with one another. I analyzed these connections using social network analysis (SNA).[6] To minimize confusion, I use plain language to describe these analyses whenever possible, supplemented by infographics and other figures. More detailed methodological information can be found in the technical appendix.

Figure 4.1 summarizes the five key features of the Tea Party website network. The first two are the foundational components of the network as a whole: the Tea Party websites and their linked organizations. To be included in this list, a Tea Party website had to meet two conditions. It had to have an active online presence between May 2012 and May 2014 (the faction's heyday), and it had to link to at least one outside organization's website. In total, 665 Tea Party groups met these conditions. The 665 Tea Party groups linked to 5,521 unique organizational websites, out of a total of 12,284 outgoing links.

To give a sense of the network's overall structure, I narrow in on our example from earlier: the eleven Tea Party groups that were active in Virginia's 7th congressional district during the period leading up to

Characterizing divisions in the Tea Party network

665 local Tea Party group websites
Each was geocoded by congressional district and
state. These Tea Party groups linked to

5,521 organizations' websites
Total of 12,284 links.

Algorithm detected 270 clusters in the network
These are referred to as "communities" in network
analysis.

**88 percent of these clusters corresponded with
the Tea Party's state and local focus**
Clusters were classified as state and local or as
national based on the locations of the groups and
organizations in the cluster.

Q
**20 organizations received links from 50 or more
Tea Party groups**
In contrast, the average website in the network was linked
to by four or fewer Tea Party groups.

FIGURE 4.1. Key attributes of the Tea Party website network

David Brat's 2014 defeat of Eric Cantor. These groups were the Constitutional Tea Party, the Chesterfield Taxpayers Alliance, the Fredericksburg Virginia Patriots, the Mechanicsville Tea Party, the New Kent Tea Party, the Patrick Henry Tea Party, the Richmond Tea Party, the Richmond Area Tea Party, the West Henrico Tea Party, the Goochland Tea Party, and the King William County Tea Party. Figure 4.2 shows the Tea Party groups in a large dark font, and the other organizations they link to in a small light font. The lines connecting Tea Party groups to other organizations represent links on the Tea Party groups' websites.

This snapshot helps us understand the connectivity among the Tea Party groups in Virginia's 7th, as well as their connections to other organizations. Five of the groups—the Constitutional Tea Party, the Mechanicsville Tea Party, the Richmond Tea Party, the Fredericksburg Virginia Patriots, and the Essex Tea Party—had lots of connections to outside organizations and to other Virginia Tea Party groups. The others were mainly connected to the network by linking to one another's pages (as were the West Henrico Tea Party, the Richmond Area Tea Party, the Goochland Tea Party, the New Kent Tea Party, and the Patrick Henry Tea Party). The final two, the King William County Tea Party and the Chesterfield Taxpayers Alliance, were connected to the other groups through other organizations or additional nearby Tea Party groups. No group was more than three degrees of separation from another group in the area, showing a pattern of regional coordination that characterized the rest of the network as well.

The remaining three features of the network (figure 4.1) each relate to the relationship between Tea Party groups and the organizations they linked to on their websites. The third component addresses the internal structure of this network and, in particular, whether there were distinct clusters of Tea Party groups that tended to link to the same organizational websites. In network analysis, these clusters are known as "communities" and are detected using a community detection algorithm that generates a list of groups that shared many links in common with one another (both sending and receiving), and fewer links in common with other groups (each website can only be a member of one community). In this network, the community detection algorithm generated 270 dis-

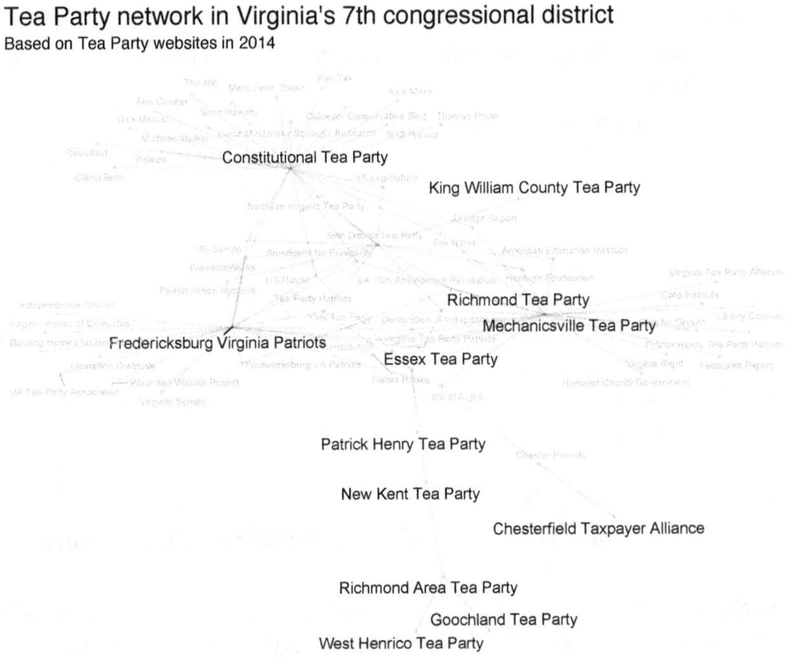

Tea Party network in Virginia's 7th congressional district
Based on Tea Party websites in 2014

Constitutional Tea Party

King William County Tea Party

Richmond Tea Party

Mechanicsville Tea Party

Fredericksburg Virginia Patriots

Essex Tea Party

Patrick Henry Tea Party

New Kent Tea Party

Chesterfield Taxpayer Alliance

Richmond Area Tea Party

Goochland Tea Party

West Henrico Tea Party

FIGURE 4.2. This close-up of one congressional district in the Tea Party website network illustrates patterns between Tea Party groups and other organizations.

tinct communities, ranging in size from communities of two (i.e., one Tea Party group that linked to only one website) to one made up of 1,615 Tea Party groups and websites.[7] Most of the communities are smaller, containing fewer than one hundred websites, while seven are large, containing more than one hundred.

The fourth component from figure 4.1 is a classification of these communities as nationally focused or locally focused, on the basis of organizations linked to in each community (this will be discussed in more detail later). The fifth and final component concerns the power dynamics in the network. We recall that Tea Party groups linked to 5,521 unique outside websites. Neither this raw number nor analysis of the divisions in the network tell us much about the relative popularity or influence of these websites, however. To understand this, I use another SNA statistic: centrality.[8] Centrality is calculated in a relatively straightforward way: a central website is one that receives proportionally more links than other websites. In this network, the average website received four links or fewer from Tea Party groups, but twenty websites received between 50 and 237 links. Examining these twenty most central, or "top-linked," websites will help us answer questions about information leadership in the Tea Party.

The remainder of this chapter uses the Tea Party's website network to extract insights about its organization. The Tea Party organization that emerges is very similar to the federated structure of a major party, in keeping with the expectation that an insurgent faction would mimic the structure of the host it is attempting to take over. This exploration begins at the top, examining which national organizations and figures local Tea Parties looked to for leadership. I then discuss the state and local patterns in the divisions (e.g., communities) that exist in the network. Finally, I draw out the political characteristics of the localities where Tea Parties were most likely to form.

Power Dynamics: An Alternative Information Infrastructure

If the Tea Party really were an insurgent faction, attempting to win control of its host party's electoral machinery wherever possible, then we might expect it to imitate the Republican Party's leadership structure as well. In other words, we should be looking for a group of voices that broadly represented the Tea Party coalition, rather than trying to

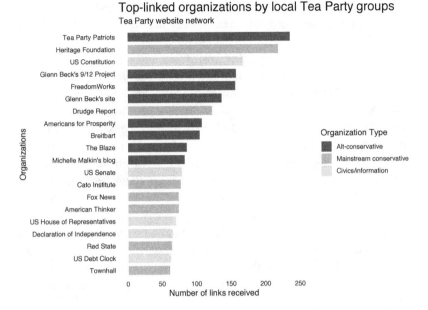

FIGURE 4.3. The most popular websites in the Tea Party network belonged to a combination of alternative conservative groups, mainstream conservative organizations, and civic resources.

identify a single voice. We can look to the Tea Party network for clues about who local Tea Party groups looked to for leadership. As noted earlier, of the 5,521 unique websites in the network, most were only linked to between one and four times—frequently by Tea Party groups in the same locality or state. But 20 of these 5,521 websites stood apart from the rest, receiving links from between 50 and 237 of the 665 local Tea Party groups. These top-linked websites are key to understanding leadership in the Tea Party.

Figure 4.3 displays these top-linked websites in order of the number of links received. Each bar corresponds with an organization, and shows how many Tea Party groups linked to that particular organization's website. As we can see, the most popular of these top-linked organizations, Tea Party Patriots, was linked to by 237 Tea Party groups, while the twentieth most popular, Townhall (a blog of the Heritage Foundation), was linked to by just over 50 Tea Party groups. The bars are also colored in three shades based on the organization's general focus. Those that represent an alternative vision of conservatism (often explicitly related to the Tea Party) are colored in black, those that correspond with more mainstream conservative organizations are in dark grey, and those that are strictly informational are in light grey.

Perhaps not surprisingly, the most dominant national voices in the network were organizations that had a clear association with the Tea Party. Tea Party Patriots, Glenn Beck's 9/12 Project, FreedomWorks, and Americans for Prosperity were four of the largest national Tea Party umbrella organizations, and their dominance is reflected in this network (they rank first, fourth, fifth, and eighth in popularity respectively). Other top resources, such as Glenn Beck himself, his network The Blaze, the conservative website Breitbart (later brought to notoriety by Trump advisor Steve Bannon), and the blogger Michelle Malkin were strongly associated with the Tea Party movement. Of course, not all Tea Party groups listened to these national groups, and many, as discussed in the previous chapter, tried to proclaim their independence from them. But when Tea Partiers did choose to turn their attention to elites, they turned to a set of groups and figures outside of the conservative mainstream.

A smaller group of top-linked organizations were more in line with the conservative mainstream: the Heritage Foundation (and Townhall, a blog run by Heritage), the Drudge Report, the Cato Institute (though more libertarian than conservative), American Thinker, Fox News, and Red State. The prominence of these organizations is in line with what we would expect from a conservative faction within the Republican Party. These organizations predated the Tea Party and enjoyed a wider Republican following, but were also friendly to the Tea Party, even providing—in the case of Fox News—a platform that allowed Tea Party messaging to reach a wider audience.

The final set of top-linked websites—civic and informational—convey more about how local Tea Party groups conceived their mission than about where they looked for leadership. The third most linked website for Tea Party groups was constitutionus.com, a page giving the text of the US Constitution. The other informational websites belonged to the Declaration of Independence, the US Senate, the US House of Representatives, and a debt counter. The appearance of these civic and informational sites in the top-linked lists corresponds with the Tea Party's purported devotion to upholding the Constitution (discussed more in the next chapter), and their commitment to keeping elected officials accountable.

These twenty top-linked groups give us an idea of where the faction looked for information. But what of the other 5,501 websites linked to by Tea Party groups, and of the divisions noted in figure 4.1? The answer to both questions is the same: the seeming divisions in the network actually correspond with the tendency of Tea Party groups to predominantly link to websites focused on their locality or region. I demonstrate this and then narrow in on the geographic locations of the Tea Party groups themselves, examining where such groups were most likely to form and why.

Regional Divisions: A Federated Structure

The overarching structure of the Tea Party's apparatus was very similar to that of the party it sought to infiltrate.[9] The Tea Party looked to a set of national leaders, yes, but it mainly waged its insurgency on the ground through a variety of outposts at state and local levels. Figure 4.4 gives a general breakdown of this federated structure, and will provide a background for the analysis that follows.

Tea Party network structure

National

- 12 percent of communities in the network were primarily made up of national organizations and public figures.

State

- 88 percent of communities in the network contained state-based organizations.
- Example: Ohio community made up of websites like Ohioans Against Common Core, Ohio Liberty Coalition, Ohio Precinct Project, Ohio Voter Integrity Project, etc.

Local

- Most state-based communities were specific to a local area such as a county or a congressional district.
- Example: In Ohio, distinct communities exist for Hocking County, Wayne County, Clinton County, and Cuyahoga County.

FIGURE 4.4. Patterns in the Tea Party website network suggest that it mimicked the organization of its host, the Republican Party.

The 270 communities in the network corresponded with three general levels of organization—national, state, and local—suggesting that the Tea Party's apparatus was very similar to that of the party it sought to infiltrate. The majority of these clusters (238 out of 270) were based in a single state or locality. I determined this by combining the community membership lists with the following metadata: the location of Tea Party groups, the location of the organizations they linked to (when available), and the focus of each organization (national or regional). I then classified each community on the basis of the location or focus of the majority of groups and organizations in that structure.[10] For example, if a cluster contained nationally-focused interest groups and statewide Tea Party umbrella organizations (like the VATPPF, mentioned in chapter 3), then I classified that community as *national*. If the majority of organizations and Tea Party groups in a community were specific to the same town, county, or state, I classified that community as *state and local*.

Thirty-two (roughly 12 percent) of the communities in the network were made up of the websites of organizations, public figures, or informational sites aimed at a national audience, and Tea Party groups that linked to these sites. Many of the websites in these communities belonged to high-profile national organizations and figures, such as the Heritage Foundation and Glenn Beck, and the Tea Party groups in these communities were often from more metropolitan areas and/or represented statewide Tea Party umbrella associations.

The remaining 237 (88 percent) of the 270 communities were specific to a single state. Figure 4.5 shows the distribution of these groups across the continental United States (though not pictured, Alaska had one such community, and Hawaii had two). As can be seen in the map, states that were more populous, or which contained a greater number of distinct metropolitan areas, such as Texas and California, tended to have more communities (indicated by darker shading). States in the Great Lakes region and points east also tended to have more Tea Party groups. The less populated states in the plains and in the mountain West hosted fewer communities, as did highly conservative states like Utah and Mississippi (indicated by lighter shading).

Not only were most of the communities focused on one state; many were specific to a certain locality within that state (e.g., a county, city, or congressional district). Figure 4.6 provides a closer look at a locally focused community: the one in Hood County, a suburb of the Dallas–Fort Worth area in Texas. This community was representative of most

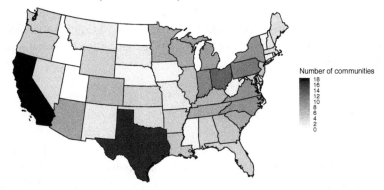

Number of Tea Party communities by state

Number of communities

18
16
14
12
10
8
6
4
2
0

FIGURE 4.5. Most Tea Party communities were based in one state. States with higher populations or more metropolitan centers tended to have more communities.

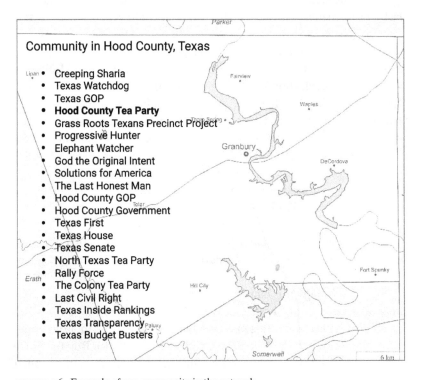

Community in Hood County, Texas

- Creeping Sharia
- Texas Watchdog
- Texas GOP
- **Hood County Tea Party**
- Grass Roots Texans Precinct Project
- Progressive Hunter
- Elephant Watcher
- God the Original Intent
- Solutions for America
- The Last Honest Man
- Hood County GOP
- Hood County Government
- Texas First
- Texas House
- Texas Senate
- North Texas Tea Party
- Rally Force
- The Colony Tea Party
- Last Civil Right
- Texas Inside Rankings
- Texas Transparency
- Texas Budget Busters

FIGURE 4.6. Example of one community in the network.

of the regional communities in the network. It contained three area Tea Party groups—the Hood County Tea Party, the North Texas Tea Party, and the Colony Tea Party—and a variety of Hood County and Texas-related organizations. Most of the regional communities followed a similar pattern.

The Structure of an Insurgency?

This network analysis has taken us a long way in understanding the relationship between local Tea Party groups and outside organizations. Indeed, what this analysis uncovered—a few influential voices at the national level combined with a robust state and local apparatus—bears many similarities to the organization of a major political party. Yet these similarities do not necessarily mean that the Tea Party was an insurgent faction in the Republican Party. The regional dispersion of Tea Party groups could stem from something far more quotidian, such as a general lack of organization within the Tea Party. It could also represent a systematic contestation of the Republican Party. To disentangle these factors, I examine *where* Tea Party groups were most likely to mobilize.

If the Tea Party was an insurgent faction, then we should observe a heavier concentration of Tea Party groups in areas that were more Republican—that is, where the Tea Party could unseat incumbent Republicans in primary elections and use the party's organizational apparatus. If the Tea Party were anything else—from a disorganized protest movement to a virulently anti-Obama wing of the Republican Party—then we ought to observe either *no* pattern in the areas where it mobilized, or a higher propensity to mobilize in Democratic areas.

To begin, I map Tea Party groups by congressional district. I then explore the relationship betweenTea Party mobilization and two district-level characteristics: the party identification of the district's US House representative, and the district's partisan leaning in the 2012 presidential election.

Figure 4.7 maps the number of local Tea Party groups in the continental United States by congressional district. As in the map of Tea Party communities (figure 4.5), more Tea Parties existed in more populous states (e.g., Texas, California, Ohio, and New York). But Tea Party groups were not spread out evenly within each state. Rather, they tended

Number of Tea Party groups by congressional district

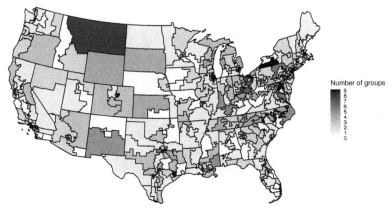

FIGURE 4.7. Within states, Tea Parties clustered in Republican congressional districts.

to cluster in a few congressional districts within a given state, particularly in Republican districts. For example, the bulk of Tea Party groups in New York were in its upstate 23rd congressional district, and the majority in California were concentrated in its 46th and 48th congressional districts (in Orange County).

This visual evidence points in the right direction, but a more systematic investigation of the correlation between district partisanship and Tea Party group concentration is in order. If the Tea Party was indeed an insurgent faction, using a contestational strategy to take over the Republican Party, then Tea Party groups should have been more likely to form in Republican districts.

Figure 4.8 helps us assess whether Tea Party groups were more likely to mobilize and remain active in districts with Republican representatives to the US House during the 113th Congress. There, the *x*-axis corresponds with the number of Tea Party groups in a district, ranging from the least (zero) to the most (nine). A light grey density curve shows the proportion of Republican districts that contained a given number of Tea party groups, and a dark grey curve shows the same for Democrats. The average Democratic district contained one or fewer Tea Party groups (a mean of 0.8). Only a handful of such districts contained between two and four groups, and only two contained more than four. The average Republican district, in contrast, contained two Tea Party groups,

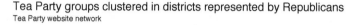

Tea Party groups clustered in districts represented by Republicans
Tea Party website network

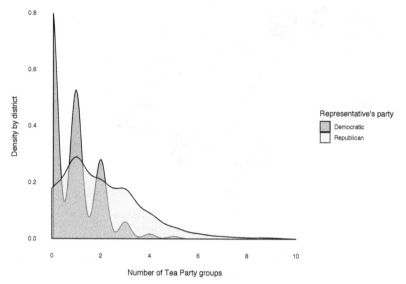

FIGURE 4.8. Tea Party groups concentrated in more Republican areas of their states, as measured by the party affiliation of each district's representative to the US House.

while many contained between three and nine. These results are consistent with an insurgent strategy of contesting Republicans in Republican districts.

We can also examine the correlation between Tea Party groups and district-level partisanship using a more nuanced measure: the proportion of a district that voted for the Republican candidate (Mitt Romney) in the 2012 presidential election. Also known as presidential vote share, this metric allows for an assessment of *how* Republican or Democratic a district was.

Figure 4.9 depicts the relationship between a district's 2012 Republican presidential vote share (on the *x*-axis, with a vertical line marking the 50-percent vote margin), and the number of Tea Party groups in that district (districts are shown as dots). For example, a dot that aligns with the 50-percent mark on the *x*-axis and the 9 mark on the *y*-axis represents a district that was a toss-up in 2012 and was home to nine Tea Party groups. Again, more reliably Republican districts contained

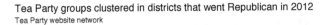

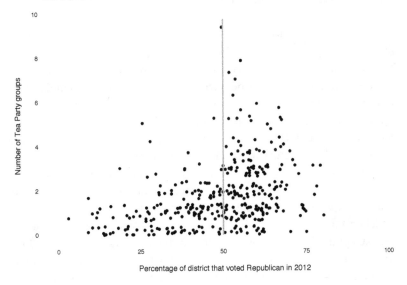

FIGURE 4.9. Tea Party groups concentrated in more Republican areas of their states, as measured by the percentage of their districts that voted for Romney in the 2012 presidential election.

more Tea Party groups, but this relationship was not monotonic. The number of Tea Party groups spiked in districts that went Republican by a 60-percent margin, but dropped off again in extremely conservative districts (districts with 40 and 80 percent of Republican vote share had similar numbers of Tea Party groups).

The takeaway is that Tea Party groups were most likely to mobilize in slightly Republican districts (those that went Republican in 2012 by 50 to 60 percent). There are several explanations for this, all of which square with what we might expect from an insurgent faction. Taking over the Republican Party's machinery would make little sense if a Republican candidate could never be expected to win in that district. But primary challenges would also be less likely to influence the Republican Party's behavior if a district was too reliably Republican. In marginally Republican districts, Tea Party groups could pose a credible threat to establishment Republicans, as failure to nominate a Tea Partier or capitulate to Tea Party demands could result in a general election loss to a Democrat.

Insurgent Organization in Review

This analysis yields two insights into how the Tea Party waged its insurgency. Starting at the top: Although the Tea Party was not united behind a single leader, Tea Party groups generally listened to the same set of elite voices. These voices belonged to Tea Party–affiliated individuals and umbrella groups (some of which figured prominently in the administration of Donald Trump, as did Breitbart's Steve Bannon). The presence of generically conservative elites in the list confirms that the Tea Party was indeed a creature of the right, and the dominance of civic resources underscores the Tea Party's mission as one of political change. Tea Partiers did not simply want to listen to elites talk about important issues; they also acted through political channels on these issues.

Second, analysis of the Tea Party website network revealed a federated structure. The divisions detected in the network corresponded not with any ideological fractionalization, but with the state and local organization of the Tea Party. Local Tea Party groups mimicked the organization of the party they sought to take over, just as we might expect from an insurgency. Despite their lack of central direction, Tea Party groups mobilized in similar congressional districts, taking advantage of similar regional, state, and local opportunities. Viewing the Tea Party as an insurgent faction allows us to make sense of this collective action paradox. A party faction arises when a group or set of groups in a party's coalition demands change from its party. An insurgent faction, characterized by its demands for partywide change and its use of confrontational strategies to enforce these demands, can be understood as the result of persistent discontent within a party coalition. The Republicans who became Tea Partiers had likely been disgruntled for some time, needing only the slightest encouragement to launch their insurgency.

But what exactly was the Tea Party demanding from the Republican Party? The next chapter examines its ideological priorities, explaining how they differed from mainstream conservatism, and thus why they sparked mobilization.

CHAPTER FIVE

Renegotiating the Terms: The Tea Party's Ideological Demands

The Tea Party is just people fighting for a way of life that's lost. It started with taxes, but now it's blossomed. — Linda R., Bucks County (Pennsylvania) Tea Party activist, interviewed May 5, 2013

In 2009 we realized we were in trouble. People who identified themselves as conservatives and constitutionalists had always been sitting down, quiet, marginalized, and victimized. They finally stood up because they felt the push of the accelerator. People were being told they were going to fundamentally change America and the concept that America was founded on. —Yvonne Donnelly, leader of Glenn Beck's 9/12 Project, interviewed September 8, 2013

As soon as it became apparent that the Tea Party was a force to be reckoned with, scholars and journalists alike set out to discover the core beliefs of Tea Partiers. Early on, David Campbell and Robert Putnam uncovered high levels of religiosity among Tea Party sympathizers, leading some to question whether the Tea Party was the Christian Right in disguise.[1] Conversely, libertarians from organizations like Freedom-Works and the Cato Institute took issue with these accusations of social conservatism, hoping that the Tea Party would exercise a "functionally libertarian" influence on the Republican Party.[2] Others, such as Alan Abramowitz, Theda Skocpol, and Vanessa Willamson, described Tea Party beliefs as more intensely conservative than those of most Republicans.[3] In other words, Tea Partiers shared the social and economic ideological commitments of the Republican Party. The real difference between Tea Partiers and others on the right stemmed from something else entirely: distrust. Tea Partiers were fundamentally suspicious of anyone or anything they perceived as threatening, including liberals (who were trying to erode the Constitution), the United Nations' Agenda 21 (a global plot to suppress property rights),[4] the news media (spreading leftist lies), Muslims (all of whom were terrorists or were attempting to impose sharia law on Americans), and immigrants (all of whom were lawless criminals).

This distrust stemmed from a different style of conservatism: *reactionary* conservatism. As Parker and Barreto argued in their 2013 study, Tea Party sympathizers were driven by a desire to take their country back—a disposition rooted in reactionary conservatism. Like traditional conservatism, reactionary conservatism prizes preservation over change. But the two ideologies differ subtly on what ought to be preserved, how change ought to be interpreted, and how conservatives ought to respond to change. Reactionary conservatives see change as a threat to their perceived cultural and social dominance. In an attempt to preserve this dominance, reactionaries are more willing to respond in procedurally radical ways.[5]

The 2016 election of Donald Trump suggested that this reactionary style had gained traction beyond the Tea Party. Voters who enthusiastically supported Trump were distinguished from other Republicans by their penchant to view ethnic and cultural outsiders as threats to their own status in American society.[6] Of course, the Tea Party was not solely responsible for the right's shift toward reactionary conservatism. Many of the voters with whom Trump resonated had likely been viewing politics for some time in terms of threats to their dominance and identity, just as reactionary conservatism has long been an undercurrent on the right. Rather, the Tea Party gave a sense of *permission* to those who wanted to bring racist, misogynist, xenophobic, hostile, anti-elitist, and any other manner of us-versus-them rhetoric into Republican Party politics, and eventually into national political conversations.

This chapter explains how the Tea Party translated a general reaction to status threats into the language of contemporary Republican conservatism. I begin by describing how an insurgent faction can renegotiate its party's ideological consensus. I then draw on a combination of activist interviews, group mission statements, and blog posts to present Tea Partiers' demands in their own words.

Party Renegotiations

The last several decades have seen the realignment of US parties along a left-right ideological dimension. Partisans have become polarized on a range of issues including race, social policies, and economics.[7] The result: two parties that correspond with conservative and liberal ideologies.

The content of these party ideologies is far from coherent. As Hans Noel explained in *Political Parties and Politcial Ideology in America*, what we know as Republican conservatism and Democratic liberalism are actually packages of issue positions that reflect the priorities of influential groups in each party's coalition.[8] What we might think of as the Republican Party's conservative commitments (e.g., resisting recognition of racial inequalities, supporting the dictates of religious traditionalism on social issues, and advocating for decreases in government spending) are simply a package of positions on which the Republican coalition agrees. Similarly, to say that the Democratic Party advances liberal positions (e.g., supporting racial equality, advocating for the rights of minority groups, and attempting to preserve the legacy of the New Deal) is to say that the Democratic coalition has reached agreement on which issues constitute liberalism.[9]

A party's ideology, then, is not set in stone. It reflects the priorities of a party coalition at a given time. Nor are party coalitions fixed. The groups that wield influence within a party evolve, and hence so do that party's priorities. Typically, this takes place in routine negotiations over which candidates or policy stances best reflect the coalitions' priorities. Some groups will benefit more from these negotiations than others, and some groups may not benefit at all. Groups who are unable to gain concessions in these routine negotiations will benefit from nothing short of a renegotiation of that package. Such a renegotiation may be difficult for any group to achieve alone, but possible for groups that join forces as a faction.

A faction, as defined in this book, is a coalition of low-influence groups that seek to gain influence in their party by any means necessary. In renegotiating its members' standing in the coalition, a faction can trigger abrupt changes in a party's issue priorities, and hence its ideology. This is exactly what happened in the case of the Tea Party. It repackaged Republican conservatism to prioritize things like immigration, law and order, and anti-elitism over economics and social issues, and relentlessly punished Republicans who did not adhere to these priorities.

But what were the Tea Party's priorities, and how did they differ from those of their host party? At the time of the Tea Party, Republican conservatism still reflected the party's most recent ideological renegotiation, at the hands of the Christian Right. In the 1980s this faction fought to incorporate religious issues into the Republican Party's ideological consensus. The Christian Right succeeded not only in renegotiating the Republican ideological consensus, but also in fomenting a decade of strife known as the "Culture Wars." During the 1990s, the two parties increasingly clashed on social issues such as abortion, school prayer, and marriage. During the Culture War years, conservative positions on economics and foreign policy were still part of the party's ideological consensus, but paled in comparison to social issues. A successful Republican candidate did not necessarily have to address economics or foreign policy, so long as they took traditional positions on issues like abortion, school prayer, and marriage.[10]

Both the country and younger members of the Republican Party had begun to liberalize on social issues by the 2000s, resulting in an unraveling of the conservative ideological priority structure.[11] By 2008, it seemed that economic issues were gaining ascendance over social issues in the party's priority structure. Indeed, the early Tea Party movement was painted as a reaction to the fiscal excesses of the Bush-era Republican Party, an image bolstered by the Tea Party's connections to libertarian politicians and organizations.[12] Yet studies of Tea Party members repeatedly suggested that the Tea Party's primary emphasis was on cultural threats, not on fiscal concerns.[13]

The Republican presidential nomination and ensuing election of Donald Trump, a candidate whose conservatism on economic and social issues was suspect at best, made the presence of a conservatism animated by cultural threat impossible to ignore. As I show in this chapter, the Tea Party revived an opposition to racial and cultural outgroups that the post-realignment Republican Party had attempted to quash. The Republican coalition had long contained groups—from the McCarthyites and the America Firsters of the 1950s to the John Birch Society and Goldwater supporters of the 1960s, to the Southern Democrats turned Reagan Republicans of the 1980s—for whom conservatism meant reaction to threats. Although reactionary conservatives did not necessarily disagree with the party's positions on economics or social issues, they prioritized these issues only inasmuch as they were connected to status or identity threat.[14]

Similarly, Tea Partiers' views on topics such as limited government, the Constitution, fiscal conservatism, and accountability did not reflect a commitment to libertarianism. Its economic emphases reflected a perception that elite institutions, liberals, welfare recipients, and immigrants threatened the dominance of middle-class white Americans. Similarly, Tea Partiers' opposition to marriage equality and transgender restrooms stemmed from a suspicion of nontraditional lifestyles, not from the dictates of religious conservatism. The combination of all this was a justification for viewing elites and cultural outgroups as threats—something many Republican voters found intuitively appealing.

Uncovering the Tea Party's Ideology

In their interviews, Tea Partiers distanced themselves from national Tea Party organizations such as FreedomWorks and Americans for Prosperity, claiming that those groups were mouthpieces of elite political insiders. In a sense, the Tea Partiers were correct. Early on, the Kochs, a family of prominent libertarian donors, had used those organizations to channel the Tea Party's protest energy into something more lasting. FreedomWorks and Americans for Prosperity had provided the fledgling Tea Party with branding, funding, and training.[15]

In *Give Us Liberty: A Tea Party Manifesto*, Freedomworks leaders Dick Armey and Matt Kibbe claimed that their organization had begun strategizing about using the "guerilla" tactics of the leftist organizer Saul Alinsky to further the cause of taxpayer activism "years before the emergence of the modern Tea Party movement." When CNBC's Rick Santelli made his televised call for the formation of a Tea Party on February 24, 2009, FreedomWorks was ready. It set up a website called "IAmWithRick.com" to give nascent activists information about organizing, and used social media and Google Maps to help organize and plan "dozens of taxpayer tea parties across the US."[16] Shortly thereafter, FreedomWorks and like-minded organizations helped activists create local groups, whom they supplied with educational materials on libertarianism and activism, such as a video series on free-market economics by Milton Friedman, Friederich Hayek's *Road to Serfdom*, and liberal organizer Saul Alinsky's *Rules for Radicals*.

As the Tea Party became involved in electoral politics, it grew increasingly apparent that most Tea Partiers were not actually committed to fiscally limited government. They found it perfectly acceptable for the government to protect their white cultural dominance, traditional lifestyles, and national boundaries. Indeed, by the 2010 midterm elections, the Kochs and other libertarians had begun to distance themselves from the Tea Party.[17] As Bill Redpath, a key official in the national Libertarian Party and the Libertarian Party of Virginia (among other offices, Redpath had been the sixteenth chair of the Libertarian Party National Committee), explained in our 2013 interview, "There are some libertarians in the Tea Party, but they're a small minority." By election day 2010, he recalled, there was an undeniable "disconnect between the Tea Party's smaller government rhetoric and how their behavior comes out," namely "their chilling use of the word 'patriot'" and their "deification of the Constitution." To libertarians, he explained, it was "frustrating to see the Tea Party come along and get all of the publicity," especially because "the Tea Party was too wrapped up in symbolism to be serious about addressing the problems of the nation."[18]

Local Tea Party groups were not alarmed by the loss of support from their former patrons. Tea Partiers were generally suspicious of "astroturf" organizations (i.e., those with DC offices, ties to the national Republican Party, or funding from big-time donors), viewing them as part and parcel of the establishment that the "grassroots" Tea Party sought to subvert. After 2010, most local groups distanced themselves from national Tea Party groups like FreedomWorks, Americans for Prosperity, Tea Party Nation, and the Tea Party Express. There was one exception: the Tea Party Patriots. Unlike the other national Tea Party organizations, the Tea Party Patriots had activist roots. The group was founded by Georgia mom Jenny Beth Martin, a former Republican campaign consultant. Martin ran a "mommy blog" about her family's struggles following the 2008 financial crisis, but after Santelli's call for a Tea Party on February 24, 2009, she turned her political experience and Internet savvy in a different direction. In March 2009 Martin created a social media page (using the platform Ning) to help Tea Party sympathizers organize and find local groups. With the help of FreedomWorks's Dick Armey, she built this social media page into the Tea Party Patriots.

Although the Tea Party Patriots maintained its identity as a "grassroots" umbrella organization, its motto "Fiscal responsibility, limited government, and free markets" reflected FreedomWorks's emphasis on economic issues. For Martin, this fiscal emphasis was strategic: "We found that so many organizations existed to deal with social issues that we didn't need another. Homosexuality, life, and other social issues are simply a way for politicians to divide us as a people while they're pulling money out of our back pockets." She saw the Tea Party Patriots' focus on "helping people take action on fiscal and economic issues" as a way to avoid those pitfalls. When asked for her own interpretation of the Tea Party Patriots' motto, Martin switched to symbolic language about the US Constitution, saying: "We look to the Constitution to see if legislation is constitutional and to see if candidates will protect the Constitution and pass constitutional legislation."

Following the Tea Party Patriots' example, activists emphasized that the Tea Party was not about social issues. But, like Martin, many Tea Partiers often defaulted to symbolic language when describing what the Tea Party *did* stand for. In the words of Colorado Tea Party leader Regina T., some local groups had "a strong faith component," but "limited government, personal responsibility, and economic freedom unite people across organizations." Brian S. of Bucks County, Pennsylvania, listed different principles: "The unity in the Tea Party, or its motif, is respect for individualism and personal responsibility, but emphases in local groups vary." Paul T. recounted how, as leader of the Mississippi state Tea Party organization, he had encouraged local groups "to focus on constitutional fidelity, fiscal responsibility, and personal responsibility," reasoning that if the Tea Party focused on these three things rather than on "other emphases," the rest would "take care of itself."

Activists framed their views using the language of fiscal conservatism, limited government, and reverence toward the Constitution. But when given the opportunity to explain their adherence to these principles, Tea Partiers used the symbolic rhetoric of fiscal conservatism to encase a set of priorities that can only be described as reactionary. In the words of Linda R., a Pennsylvania activist, "The Tea Party is just people fighting for a way of life that's lost." To Linda, the biggest threat to this way of life came from Muslims, who she believed were working through President Obama to replace the US Constitution with sharia law. She believed that "under Obama, America is under attack like it was from communism. Operatives from the Muslim Brotherhood occupy his government. He's trying to shut down religious organizations and stop conservative messages." Some activists, like Linda, focused on threats from "multiculturalism," which encompassed Muslims, immigrants, and African Americans (whom Tea Partiers referred to as the "undeserving poor" and "welfare queens"). Others were fixated on "cultural corruption," framing their objections to abortion and "gay marriage" as evidence of America's decline. Some groups championed freedom from government regulation and oversight on issues including school vouchers, natural gas fracking, taxation, local property rights, and guns. A few of the Tea Parties' emphases bordered on the conspiratorial, including beliefs that the United Nations' Agenda 21. a 1992 sustainable development initiative. was a plot to create a one-world government, or that the new Common Core school curriculum was being used to brainwash children with a "liberal agenda."

I continue this examination of Tea Partiers' ideology by looking at local groups' websites, comparing the priorities given in Tea Party groups' mission statements with the explanations of those priorities given in their blog posts. This systematic analysis of the rhetoric will reveal how the Tea Party used the symbolism of fiscal responsibility and constitutionally limited government to renegotiate the content of Republican conservatism.

Tea Party Mission Statements

Local Tea Parties summarized their core principles for the public through their mission statements, which they posted on their websites and social media pages. Most of these statements were a combination of elements from the mission statements of the Tea Party Patriots or Glenn Beck's 9/12 project (another grassroots-style umbrella organization) and the local group's policy priorities.

I collected the mission statements of the local groups that had active websites or social media pages between 2012 and 2014, a total of 1,051 Tea Party groups. To summarize these statements, I recorded the issues mentioned in a random sample of one hundred mission statements. This resulted in eighteen categories: taxes, size of government, religion/Christianity, private property, personal responsibility, anti-Obama/Democrats, individual rights, immigration, the Affordable Care Act/Obamacare, the Second Amendment / personal firearms, free markets, fiscal responsibility, distrusting the GOP, having an election mission, having an education mission, national defense, the Constitution, and keeping the government accountable. I then recorded how many statements mentioned each topic.

For example, Indy Defenders of Liberty West, a Tea Party organization located just outside Indianapolis, listed the following as their mission statement:

> To restore *limited government, fiscal responsibility,* and *accountable* representation through citizen activism and *education,* in order to preserve the *Constitution* of the United States of America [*emphasis added*].

I coded this statement as mentioning the following categories: size of government, fiscal responsibility, accountability, an educational mission, and the Constitution.

Figure 5.1 shows the most frequently mentioned issues in Tea Party mission statements. Not surprisingly, the most-mentioned topic was the US Constitution. More than half of the mission statements also mentioned the three core principles of the Tea Party Patriots: size of government, fiscal responsibility, and free markets. Given the national reach of the Tea Party Patriots and the affiliation of many local groups with

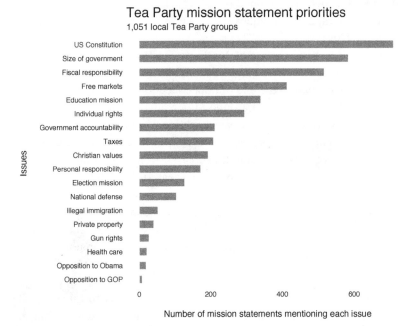

FIGURE 5.1. The official mission statements on Tea Party groups' websites tended to be vague, emphasizing the Constitution and fiscal issues.

that organization, the emphasis on constitutionally limited government and fiscal conservatism in their mission statements is not surprising. Most groups also included other principles in their mission statements. At least one-quarter of the statements emphasized education of the public, individual rights, keeping governmental officials accountable, taxes, religion/Christianity, and personal responsibility. Some also mentioned elections, national defense, illegal immigration, private property, guns, antipathy toward Obama or liberals, the Affordable Care Act, and distrust of the Republican Party.

Tea Party Blog Posts

Many Tea Party websites also maintained blogs in which local group leaders as well as rank-and-file members expressed their opinions on various issues. Unlike their mission statements, which often mimicked those of national Tea Party groups, Tea Party blog posts provide an unfiltered look at the priorities of local Tea Party groups. About two hundred local groups maintained blogs between the years 2009 and 2015. I used web-scraping techniques to extract the 42,479 posts that appeared on these blogs.

Figure 5.2 shows the arc of Tea Party groups' activity, displaying the number of posts on these blogs by month from the beginning of the Tea Party in early 2009 to the end of data collection in December 2015. The first blogs began in earnest around March 2009, during which month 95 posts were written. Blog posts were published with increasing frequency from this point until April 2013, during which 922 posts were written. The number of posts per month decreased from that point onward. By December 2015, when data collection ceased, blog activity was back down to early-2010 levels.

Spikes in blog activity generally corresponded with events of significance to the Tea Party. Several are labeled here. The first surge of activity occurred in April 2009, corresponding with the first major Tea Party protest, the Tax Day Protest. Another surge occurred in March 2010, in response to the passage of the Affordable Care Act (ACA), and again around the 2010 midterm elections. From August 2011 to July 2014, Tea Party bloggers became more prolific, responding to the debt ceiling crisis and government shutdown in August 2011, the first few Republican presidential primaries in early 2012, the first Supreme Court ruling on

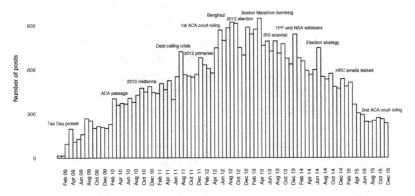

FIGURE 5.2. This timeline shows the current events that corresponded with spikes in Tea Party blog post activity.

the ACA in June 2012, the Benghazi attack in September 2012, the 2012 election, the April 2013 Boston Marathon bombing, the "scandal" involving the Internal Revenue Service's profiling of Tea Party groups in May 2013 (which remained a focus for several months afterward), Wikileaks's release of documents about the Trans-Pacific Partnership (TPP) and the National Security Agency's surveillance of citizens (both of which concerned Tea Partiers) in January 2014, and discussions of candidates and strategies for the upcoming midterm elections in July 2014. After this point, posts decreased in frequency, with a few minor surges reflecting growing interest in Secretary of State Hillary Clinton's emails beginning in late 2014, and responses to the second Supreme Court ruling on the ACA in June 2015.

Uncovering trends in the content of these posts is, however, more difficult than noting trends over time. Because this many posts (more than forty-two thousand) would be difficult or impossible to code reliably by hand, I turned to topic modeling, a form of automated (i.e. computer-assisted) content analysis that discovers the underlying topics in a set of documents, implemented through the latent dirichlet allocation, or LDA, model. The next few paragraphs include a brief description of the analysis to aid the reader in interpreting the substantive results that follow. Additional details are available in the technical appendix.

Like any form of content analysis, topic models are a means of summarizing the themes in a body of text. Unlike human coders, a topic model like LDA does not need a coding scheme, nor does it rely on background knowledge of the documents. To generate meaningful output, all a topic model needs is a corpus of documents that contain words. LDA is built on the assumption that each document can be understood structurally as a mixture of words, and that words that occur together frequently within and across documents represent a distinct topic in the corpus. It asks: What is the probability that this group of words would appear over and over again in multiple documents? If the probability is high, the model classifies that set of words as a *topic*, understood in its common English meaning as a subject discussed in a text.

Figure 5.3 depicts this process, beginning with the collection of blog posts (the corpus). I used a series of preprocessing techniques to ensure that the words in each post could be compared and analyzed by the model. This involved removing anything that would create unnecessary noise in the analysis, including punctuation and other symbols, numbers, white space, and common English stop words (e.g., "the," "and," "or"). Further, because many words can take a variety of forms, I reduced each word to its English stem. For example, the words "investigate," "investigation," and "investigator" were all reduced to their shared stem, "investig" (I include a full version of each word in my presentation of the results to enhance interpretability). After preprocessing, I used LDA to identify the one hundred topics discussed in these documents, and the words that most distinguished each topic from the others.[19]

Finally, I interpreted and assigned a label to each of the topics, on the basis of their key words. Three examples are shown in figure 5.3. I assigned the first of these the label *illegal immigration topic* because its key words were "illegal," "immigration," "security," "country," "American," "law," "enforce," "millions," and "stop." (In preprocessing, all words in the blog posts were reduced to their English roots, and capitalization was removed. The raw output thus consisted of uncapitalized word stems, which can be difficult to interpret. To aid in interpretation, I reintroduced capitalization and word endings in the word lists shown in Figure 5.4.) I labeled the second example in figure 5.3 *liberal media topic* due to its key words: "liberal," "progressive," "left," "media," "agenda," and "side." I referred to the third example, which included words like "America," "nation," "people," "historic," "great," "freedom," and "destroy," as an *American greatness topic*.

Based on these one hundred topics, Tea Party blogs had three main

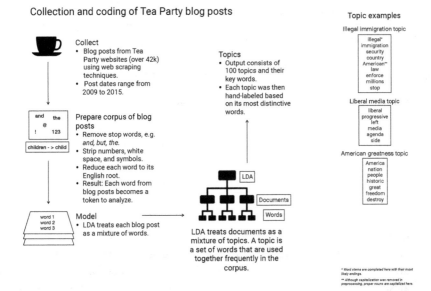

FIGURE 5.3. Summary of how automated content analysis models (e.g., LDA) classify blog posts into topics

focuses: advertising opportunities for Tea Party activism, criticism of politicians, and discussion of policy. These focuses, with a summary of topics discussed under each, are shown in table 5.1. Topics in the activism category tell us little about the Tea Party's ideology, instead reflecting Tea Party groups' use of these blogs to disseminate information about meetings, events, and canvassing efforts leading up to elections. Posts in the other two categories—criticism of politicians and discussion of policy—provide more insights into the Tea Party's ideology. What emerges is very much in line with the argument that the Tea Party sought to renegotiate Republican conservatism.

Ideological Themes: Distrust and Threats

In figure 5.4, I list the most representative topics in the politician and policy categories. There, each box contains one topic. The label I assigned to that topic is displayed first in a larger font, followed by the key words that the LDA model associated with that topic (when referring to key words in the text, I use italics). Readers are encouraged to examine and interpret these topics on their own, keeping the the following in

TABLE 5.1. **Tea Party blog post focuses**

Blog post focuses	Topics discussed
Advertisement of activism	Tea Party meetings and events Civic activism (get-out-the-vote efforts) Local political issues
Criticism of politicians	Criticism of GOP establishment Criticism of Obama Criticism of other Democrats or liberals
Discussion of policy	Government spending and economic issues Social issues Law and order (policing, immigration) Other policy areas (health care, education, social security)

mind. For a topic to emerge from the model, multiple blog posts had to mention the same thing, using the same language. Stated otherwise, of all the issues Tea Partiers could have discussed on their blogs, they coalesced around these issues and not others; and of all the words Tea Partiers could have used to discuss these issues, they tended to converge on these words and not others.

Topics in the first two columns of figure 5.4 relate to politicians. Of these, one features criticism of *establishment* Republicans in Washington for their lack of *conservative leadership* or *principles*. Three others pertain to governmental actors generally, including a topic on the *problems* with *special interests*, one on placing *term limits* on *time* in office, and another on the *government's violations* of *states' rights* and the *Constitution*.

The final three topics in the politicians category target Democrats and liberals. When discussing Obama, Tea Party blog posts emphasized his *failure* to keep his *promises*. Tea Partiers also singled out Obama's attorney general, Eric Holder, calling for an *investigation* and *criminal charges*. (Holder was persona non grata to the movement for declining to hand over information about the Fast and Furious investigation, for refusing to defend the Defense of Marriage Act, and for not defending Tea Party groups against unfair treatment from the IRS.) In another topic, Tea Partiers criticized the *liberal media* for having a *progressive agenda*, and for being on the other *side* (something Donald Trump would later echo in charges of "fake news").

These topics reflect a general suspicion of elites, as discussed in chapter 3 of this book. Significantly, Tea Party blog posts did not focus

How Tea Partiers discussed politicians and policy in their blog posts

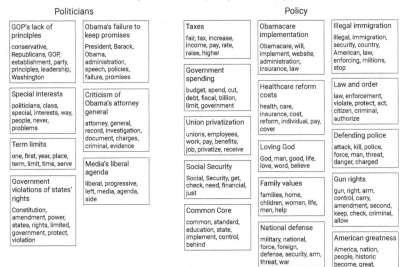

FIGURE 5.4. How Tea Partiers discussed politicians and policy in their blog posts. Each box contains one topic and its key words as discovered by LDA, as well as a descriptive label. To enhance interpretability, likely English stems and capitalization have been added to key words; these were removed during preprocessing.

solely—or even primarily—on liberals, but on criticizing established politicians more generally. When they did discuss liberals, their language bordered on conspiratorial, from the calls for criminal investigations to the emphasis on the liberal media's agenda.

The remaining three columns in figure 5.4 contain the topics from the LDA model that were most clearly about policy issues. Three of these emphasized fiscal issues. The first reflected Tea Partiers' complaints about *higher* taxes, as well as their support for the *fair tax*, a national consumption tax that would replace income and payroll taxes (Tea Partiers' support of the fair tax drove a wedge between them and other Republicans early on).[20] The other two fiscal topics were more in line with the fiscal conservative positions of the Tea Party's early libertarian backers: Tea Partiers supported *budget cuts* and other *limits* on *government spending*, as well as *privatizing unions*.

But local groups did not devote their blogs entirely, or even mainly, to fiscal issues. The remaining policy topics showcase a curious blend of conservative orthodoxy and something more reactionary. Tea Partiers' seeming opposition to government spending belied their allegiance to federal programs from which they benefited, such as Social Security. Reminiscent of the infamous "Keep your government hands off my Medicare!" sign from an early Tea Party protest, blog posts on this topic emphasized the right to Social Security, and the importance of making sure people *got* the *check* they *needed*.

Tea Partiers were much less sympathetic to the two other federal programs that received repeated mentions in their blog posts: the Common Core state standards initiative for education, and health care reform. They saw this uniform educational standard as an attempt at *state control*, and opposed its implementation. Two topics emerged on health care reform, reflecting different stages of the debate. One of these focused on the website issues that the Obama administration encountered when attempting to implement the exchanges. The other criticized the *costs* that *health care reform* would place on the *individual*. Three topics featured traditionalist rhetoric. One linked *loving* and *believing* in *God* and the Bible (the *good word*) to leading a *good life*. Another topic emphasized family values and home life. The third featured a hawkish discussion of *national defense*, calling for the *military* to *arm* itself, use *force,* and engage in *war* against *foreign threats* to the nation's *security*. Based on these topics alone, there is not much backing for the claim that the Tea Party sought to renegotiate the Republican Party's ideological priorities. Tea Partiers may have used reactionary rhetoric to discuss some of these issues, but fiscal conservatism, social security, family values, and so forth were already priorities in the Republican coalition. The basis of the Tea Party's ideological renegotiation can be found in the final five policy topics. In a preview of what would become priorities under the Republican Party of Donald Trump, Tea Partiers focused on immigration enforcement, policing, and guns as ways to protect their American identity from threats.

To begin, Tea Partiers saw illegal immigration as a threat to America's security, framing their discussion of immigration in terms of *enforcing American laws* in order to *stop* the influx of *millions* of *illegal immigrants* into the country. The next two topics showcase coded racial language. A topic on *law enforcement* and *criminals* uses the kind of law-and-order language first used by Richard Nixon to target African Americans and Vietnam War protesters.[21] In a similar vein, Tea Partiers tapped into identity threats through a different proxy: the police. Undoubtedly a response to heightened criticism of the police following the shooting of several unarmed black boys and men by white police officers between 2012 and 2015, this topic reads as a defense of police officers' use of *force* to *kill* any *man* who posed a *threat*, *charged* the officer, or in some other way put the officer in *danger*. The topic on guns and the Second Amendment suggests that Tea Partiers fear the government might *control* or not *allow* them to have guns (perhaps through policies like the *criminal* background *check*). The final topic encapsulates Tea Partiers' sense that their identity as Americans was at stake. In the kind of America-first language that became the core of Trump's campaign slogan, "Make America great again," Tea Partiers lauded the *historic greatness* of their *nation,* and decried attempts to *destroy* the *freedoms* of the American *people.*

Summary: Insurgency and Renegotiation

In their 2013 book *Change They Can't Believe In: The Tea Party and Reactionary Politics in America,* Christopher Parker and Matt Barretto analyzed a survey of Tea Party sympathizers in the mass public to argue that Tea Partiers were motivated not by libertarian ideological commitments, but by reactionary conservatism. Reactionary conservatism is an impulse to see change, especially change to one's status or way of life, as a threat.[22] This reactionary impulse has deep roots in American society, going back, at least in Parker and Barreto's estimation, to right-wing insurgencies like the Know-Nothing Party of the 1850s, the Ku Klux Klan of the 1920s, and the John Birch Society of the 1960s.

The evidence presented here corroborates Parker and Barreto's account, suggesting that the connection between reactionary conservatism and the Tea Party went all the way to the faction's activist core. Yet, the content of the Tea Party's ideology is only one part of the story. The Tea Party is hardly the first reactionary group to emerge on the right, but it is the first to insert this language into the mainstream discourse of a major party. It seems to have renegotiated Republican conservatism, prioritizing issues related to status over traditional economic or social issues, and packaging those issues with the language of threat.

This brings us back to the root of it all: party coalitions. Negotiations, ideological or otherwise, are routine in a party coalition's efforts to reach and maintain an equilibrium. Most of the time, a faction's best hope of seeing its goals realized is to accept compromises from its coalition in return for a few concessions. A faction attempts a renegotiation when it has demands that cannot be accommodated within the party's existing ideological consensus, or that it does not trust the coalition to accommodate.

I suggest that the Tea Party mobilized as an insurgent faction to force just such an ideological renegotiation. In particular, Tea Partiers sought to renegotiate the Republican Party's conservative consensus to prioritize a different package of issue positions, oriented around the perception of threat. Understanding the Tea Party's impact on the Republican Party's ideology as a renegotiation rather than, say, a realignment helps to illuminate why it continued to embrace certain core values from the previous conservative consensus, such as fiscal conservatism and limited government. A renegotiation means not that one ideological package replaces another, but simply that the content of that package—and potentially the rationale for why certain issue positions are included in the package—shifts.

In the case of the Tea Party, this meant elevating issues like immigration, guns, terrorism, law and order, and anti-elitism—all of which were undergirded by a reaction to threats—to prominent places in Republican conservatism. Further, Tea Partiers did not eschew conventionally conservative issue areas like limited government and moral traditionalism; they simply changed the rationale for including these ideas in their renegotiated conception of conservatism.

This ideological renegotiation seems to have been successful—at least so far. Recent research shows that voters and activists who supported Trump's 2016 nomination bid differed from other Republicans in their tendency to see the world in terms of status threats.[23] The Trump presidency has brought the tenets of this new conservative consensus into sharp relief. Trump's key policy proposals have all involved some violation of traditionally conservative emphases on fiscal responsibility or constitutionally limited government, including his liberal use of executive orders, his attempt to spend massive amounts of taxpayer money on a wall with Mexico, his persistent focus on limiting immigration and painting immigrants as criminals, his commitment to protectionism, his emphasis on law and order, his refusal to decry white supremacists and their supporters, his attack on the liberal media, and so on.

This chapter suggests that Trump's positions are not an anomaly, but are the result of nearly a decade of Tea Party pressure on the Republican Party. The Tea Party pressured Republicans to be accountable to its version of conservatism or face electoral punishment. By 2016 most Republicans still in office had capitulated to the Tea Party's demands in some way or another, and the fear of outsiders and distrust of elites to which Trump appealed so directly had become part and parcel of the new Republican conservative consensus.

CHAPTER SIX

Taking Over the House:
Insurgent Factions and Congress

Will the Tea Party stay? We can only hope that enough good officials are elected that we don't have to exist anymore. We have learned that we have to keep our eyes on our elected officials. — Jenny Beth Martin, leader of the Tea Party Patriots, interviewed October 24, 2012

Marking nearly every decade of the past century, dissident lawmakers have developed organizations, distinct from party institutions and other so-called congressional member associations, to secure policies opposed by party leaders. —Ruth Bloch Rubin, *Building the Bloc: Intraparty Organizations in the US Congress*

The Republican Party enjoyed widespread victories in the 2010 midterm elections, ushering in a set of freshmen representatives. Many of these newcomers received support from the Tea Party in primary contests, where they challenged and defeated established Republican candidates. Once elected, these Tea Party Republicans seemed to prefer gridlock and obstruction to compromise and cooperation, even when it came to their own party's leadership.[1] Tea Partiers' first year in the House of Representatives was marked by a protracted battle over raising the debt ceiling, in which a shutdown of the federal government was narrowly averted. Two years later, Tea Partiers put up such resistance to the implementation of Obama's Affordable Care Act that the federal government shut down from October 1 to October 17, 2013.

By September 2015, John Boehner, the Republican speaker of the House, had grown so frustrated with the "turmoil" wrought by Tea Party Republicans that he resigned from both the speakership and the House.[2] House Republicans awarded the speakership to Paul Ryan, the favored candidate of the House Freedom Caucus (HFC), which acted as a key institutional organ of the Tea Party in Congress. The message was clear: either fall in line with the Tea Party or be replaced. Yet, even under Ryan's speakership, Tea Partiers continued to prioritize remaking the Republican Party in the House over governing, and certainly over their party's reputation. After three years as speaker, Ryan followed Boehner's example, announcing that he would not seek reelection in the 2018 midterms.[3]

This kind of obstructionist behavior is relatively common in an era of polarized congressional parties—at least, from members of one party toward the other party.[4] Tea Partiers were no friends of congressional Democrats, to be sure, but they were also willing to oppose their own party no matter the cost. Their seemingly contradictory behavior was not the result of strategic naivete. Rather, it was exactly in line with the insurgent tactics they had used to take over the Republican Party at state and local levels. The US House was simply another stop in the faction's quest to expand its terrain.

In this chapter I focus on the Tea Party's mobilization in the House of Representatives. Although the House has a few features that make factions more visible than in state and local parties (namely, its set number of representatives and the existence of semiformal organizations called caucuses; more about these later), we still know relatively little about how and why a faction might attempt to commandeer its host party in government. The Tea Party provides a unique opportunity to examine why a faction might mobilize in an era of polarized congressional parties, the strategies a congressional faction can use to expand its influence beyond caucuses, and the extent to which congressional factions share the goals and strategies of their state and local counterparts. I begin by explaining what it means to conceptualize the Tea Party in Congress as an insurgent faction. Then, using data from the peak years of the Tea Party's insurgency in the House (2011–15), I address two empirical questions. First, does the behavior of House Republicans in this period correspond with a Tea Party takeover? Second, what policy priorities and rhetoric, if any, distinguished Tea Partiers from other House Republicans?

The Tea Party Faction in Congress

Congress provides the opportunity to examine the relationship between the Republican Party and the Tea Party in greater detail. This is partially related to scale. State and local parties are variable and numerous, making it difficult to discuss factions in these contexts without relying on illustrative examples (Virginia's 2013 RPV), or on generalizations (as in chapter 4). In contrast, the US House features two party organizations and 435 representatives (a number fixed in law since 1911). We know quite a bit about these representatives, including their party affiliations, their personal demographics, the characteristics of their districts, how they have voted, what they have said on the floor, what they have written in press releases, their staffs and budgets, how long they have been in Congress, and what committees they sit on. In addition, the frequency of House elections (members are up for reelection every two years), allows us to spot changes in membership and voting patterns relatively quickly.

Not only are congressional parties easier to study, but factions within them are easier to identify. This is particularly true in the House, which allows members to form caucuses, a type of legislative membership organization.[5] Caucuses represent a wide array of interests, are eligible to receive funding from the House, and have varying membership requirements. Some, such as the Congressional Bourbon Caucus, focus on extracurricular interests and are easy to join. Others, like the HFC, are selective in whom they admit as members. Some, like the former Tea Party caucus, publicize their membership list, while others, like the HFC, are more secretive. Some, such as the Blue Dog Democrats, are explicitly partisan, while others, like the Congressional Black Caucus, transcend party lines. Most important, caucuses are independent of party leadership, making them an ideal organizational tool for the occasional faction in the House.[6]

Still, most caucuses never overlap with factions, largely because factions in Congress are relatively rare. This has been especially true in the last few decades, which have seen an uptick in partisan polarization and the resurgence of strong congressional party leadership.[7] Understandably, conversations about congressional parties have focused on explaining the causes and consequences of conflict between the two parties, not with them. Yet, as growing numbers of Tea Party Republicans joined Congress, a rift emerged *within* the Republican Party. Tea Partiers in the House, like their activist counterparts, were fond of obstructionist tactics.[8] The Tea Party became the first congressional faction since Newt Gingrich's Republican Study Committee of the late 1980s to deliberately weaken its host party in order to gain concessions and control.[9]

Defining the Tea Party in Congress

Examining the Tea Party in Congress is complicated by a definitional matter: there is no straightforward way to distinguish Tea Partiers from other House Republicans. Over a six-year span (the 112th, 113th, and 114th Congresses), there were not one but *three* Tea Party–related caucuses: the Tea Party Caucus, the Liberty Caucus, and the Freedom Caucus. I summarize these briefly below.

The Tea Party Caucus. The Tea Party Caucus was formed in July 2010 by Michele Bachmann (R-MN).[10] Because it was formed before the 2010 midterm elections, which swept in the first wave of Tea Party–identifying legislators, the caucus's original membership list consisted of sitting Republican legislators with whom the Tea Party struck a chord. Its ranks swelled after the 2010 midterms, but by 2013 many of the caucus's founding members had left office or lost energy, and the caucus went dormant.[11] Because of this, the membership list of the Tea Party Caucus provides only partial information about who was part of the Tea Party faction in the House.

The Liberty Caucus. Between 2013 and 2015, Tea Partiers in the House lacked an avenue for organized action. During this period, many Tea Party–sympathetic representatives, including members of the defunct Tea Party Caucus, attended a series of lunches hosted by Ron Paul (R-TX). In 2011, this lunch series had morphed into the Liberty Caucus, which claimed kinship with the Tea Party and was even chaired by Tea Party favorite Justin Amash (R-MI).[12]

The House Freedom Caucus. The solidification of the Tea Party's presence in the House occurred in January 2015, when thirty members of the House—many of whom were veterans of the other two Tea Party–related caucuses—formed the House Freedom Caucus. Unlike the Tea Party and Liberty caucuses, the HFC was an invitation-only caucus that reserved membership for Republicans who were willing to oppose Boehner, the Republican speaker of the House. The HFC had two goals: to pressure the Republican leadership to enact a more conservative agenda, and to do so without frantic scurrying on the floor.[13] Although the HFC did not cling to the Tea Party label (very few did by 2015), it carried on the Tea Party's obstructionism.

Combining the membership information for these three caucuses provides a plausible baseline list of the key players in the Tea Party faction in the House.[14] In total, one hundred representatives who held congressional office between the 112th and the 114th Congresses were members of at least one of these caucuses. Many of these representatives were members of two or more caucuses during this time period. By design, this definition excludes legislators who enjoyed residual support by a Tea Party–related interest group during a campaign, but never officially joined a political organization linked to the Tea Party.[15] It also excludes members of the House who cooperated with the Tea Party but did not join one of the Tea Party–related caucuses.

Analyzing the Tea Party in Congress

I drew from three sources of data on the behavior of House Republicans in the 112th, 113th, and 114th Congresses. I explain these briefly here, then discuss them in more detail below. The first were roll-call voting patterns, which I analyzed by vote type. Parties in Congress, especially majority parties, usually go to great lengths to avoid disunity in their party's votes on legislation. Evidence of the Tea Party routinely voting differently from other Republicans would signal a high level of fractiousness.

Cosponsorships on legislation were the second source of data. Party leadership has substantially less influence over who cosponsors with whom, thus giving members flexibility to form connections with whomever they please. If Tea Partiers consistently cosponsored legislation with one another to the exclusion of establishment Republicans, then this would also signal fractiousness.

Finally, I examined press releases. In these, representatives can use whatever language they wish to communicate their positions and achievements on pertinent issues to an external audience—namely, their constituencies. Uncovering evidence that Tea Partiers framed issues differently from establishment Republicans would also signal a distinct faction.

Covoting and Cosponsorships

I analyzed the covoting and cosponsorship behavior of legislators separately for all three congressional sessions (the 112th, 113th, and 114th) using network analysis. Figure 6.1 uses the covoting networks as an illustration. For each session of Congress, I created three covoting net-

House Republicans' covoting networks

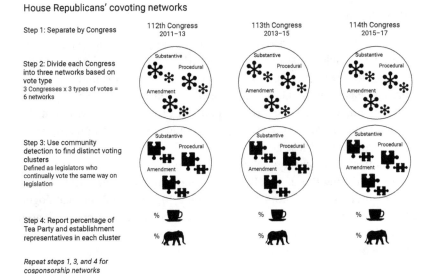

FIGURE 6.1. Explanation of the steps taken in the creation and analysis of Republican voting networks

works based on the type of vote (substantive, procedural, or final passage).[16] This resulted in six total covoting networks, three per Congress. In each network, Republicans who voted the same way on the same piece of legislation (yea or nay) are linked by that shared vote. The more votes two legislators have in common, the stronger the connection between them.

Because the real question is whether *divisions* were systematically present within the Republican Party, the third step involved determining whether such divisions existed. For this, I returned to the community detection algorithm discussed in chapter 4,[17] which assigned representatives to different groups (e.g., communities) on the basis of similarities in their voting behavior. Finally, I examined the correspondence between these communities of representatives and their Tea Party affiliation.

I analyzed legislative cosponsorships similarly, treating each congressional session as its own network, for a total of three networks. I then used a community detection algorithm to identify groups of legislators who cosponsored together frequently. Once again, I examined whether these divisions corresponded with known Tea Party legislators.

Press Releases

While data on congressional covoting and cosponsorship behavior are readily available, press releases are not. Each member of the House possesses their own House.gov web page on which they post and archive all press releases they issue. While information on covoting and cosponsorships is readily available, no repository of press releases existed at the time of data collection. Press releases could be obtained directly from each legislator's House.gov website.

I collected these press releases in two phases. First, for Republicans in office during the data collection period (late 2015 and early 2016), I wrote individualized html-based scrapers to download and catalogue their press releases. In the second phase, I collected the press releases of legislators who had been in the 112th and 113th Congresses but were no longer in office (legislators' websites are taken down once they leave office). For this, I turned to Archive.org, also known as the "Wayback Machine"—a website that archives snapshots of defunct pages. Through a laborious process, I wrote an additional set of scrapers, sometimes multiple ones per member, to extract press releases from archived versions of past members' websites. The resulting data set contained all accessible press releases issued by House Republicans (Tea Party and establishment) from 2011 through 2015, for a total of 58,750 press releases from 273 members.

Analyzing a data set of this magnitude presented a different set of problems. As with the blog posts in chapter 5, I needed an efficient way to summarize patterns in press release content. For this, I turned to automated content analysis, implemented here using the Structural Topic Model, or STM), which not only uncovers topics, but also allows the researcher to examine the relationship between these topics and other covariates of interest.[18] I focused primarily on the relationship between Tea Party caucus membership and the propensity with which certain topics were discussed. In addition, I controlled for factors that could be correlated with Tea Party membership, such as ideology, district conservatism, and year.[19]

The next two sections examine legislators' behavior in the form of covoting and cosponsorships, followed by an analysis of the rhetoric legislators use in their press releases. Throughout, I find confirmation of a distinct and increasingly influential Tea Party faction in Congress.

Takeover Behavior: Covoting and Cosponsorships

Covoting

Roll call votes on the House floor have long been among the most public and traceable actions congressional members can take. In the 1980s, Keith Poole and Howard Rosenthal used these votes to construct measures of the relative moderation or extremism of members of Congress, as well as the cohesiveness of the parties, culminating in what are now known as DW-NOMINATE scores.[20] Since then, scholars have used these scores to document increasing distance between the two parties in Congress, among other trends.[21]

These studies have yielded consensus on two points. First, the Republican and Democratic parties have grown more polarized over the last few decades. Second, congressional parties exert sizable influence over how their partisans vote, in terms of both agenda control and party discipline.[22] Taking these findings into account, we should therefore expect very little from the Tea Party in distinctive voting patterns. Instead, high levels of polarization between the two parties make it plausible that, when it comes down to voting, Tea Partiers would rally with establishment Republicans against their common enemy, the Democrats. However, I present general evidence of distinct voting patterns using aggregated ideology scores, followed by more detailed results from the covoting networks.

Figure 6.2 allows us to compare the ideological distribution of Tea Party and establishment Republicans. The ideological scores shown here are the first dimension DW-NOMINATE scores of establishment Republicans and Tea Party members. DW-NOMINATE scores are based on legislators' voting patterns. Each legislator was assigned a score that indicates their moderation or extremism relative to that of other House members, thus providing a rough approximation of legislators' ideology. The scores range from −1, the most liberal, to 1, the most conservative. As this plot shows, Tea Partiers' ideological scores were distributed more toward the conservative end of this scale than were the scores of establishment Republicans.

In the 112th Congress (January 2011 to January 2013), the average score for establishment Republicans was 0.42, in contrast to 0.57 for Tea Partiers. This gap increased during the Congresses in which the Liberty

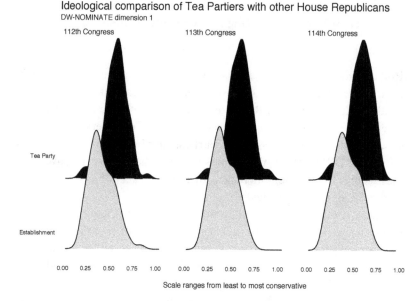

Ideological comparison of Tea Partiers with other House Republicans

FIGURE 6.2. Tea Partiers were more conservative than other Republican representatives, and this difference increased over time.

Caucus and the HFC became active, rising to a mean of 0.43 for establishment Republicans and 0.59 for Tea Partiers in the 113th (from January 2013 to January 2015), and remaining relatively steady at 0.43 for the establishment and 0.58 for Tea Partiers in the 114th (January 2015 to January 2017). This gap in the ideology scores of Tea Party and establishment Republicans is in line with findings in previous work.[23]

To see what drove this gap, I analyzed the covoting behavior of House Republicans on three key types of votes: procedural, amendment, and substantive (votes on the final passage of a bill). In the House, these different types of roll call votes reflect different stages in the legislative process and different amounts of pressure from party leadership. Party leadership often uses rules and procedures to minimize intraparty conflict on final-passage votes, or to avoid forcing members of their party to take actions that might hurt them in coming elections. Members of Congress thus vote for two different audiences: party leadership, in procedural and amendment votes, and their constituency, in final-passage votes. This means that we should expect to see some intraparty variation on substantive votes, but not as much variation on procedural or amendment votes.[24] Examining patterns across these different *types* of votes will help us distinguish whether these voting differences are simply signals to constituents or reflections of a systematically distinct mode of legislating.[25]

I used social network analysis (SNA) techniques to construct covoting networks for all three types of votes for three sessions of Congress, resulting in six total networks. Here, legislators are connected by voting the same way on the same piece of legislation. The more frequently two legislators vote together, the greater the strength of their connection. Using a community detection algorithm, I uncovered distinct voting blocs within each network. Finally, I mapped each of these communities, or blocs, onto the list of Tea Party–related caucus members. The results of these analyses are shown in figures 6.3 (substantive votes), 6.4 (procedural votes), and 6.5 (amendment votes). The bars in the graphs each correspond with a community. The number of Tea Party legislators in each community is shown by the darker shading of the bars.

Starting with figure 6.3, we can see that each Congress contained two

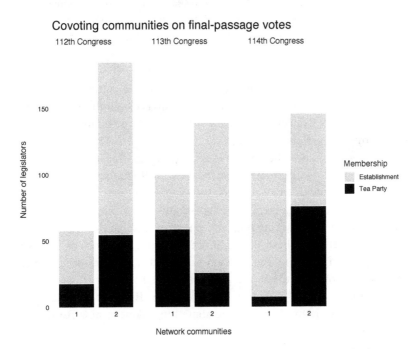

FIGURE 6.3. House Republicans increasingly shifted toward the Tea Party on final-passage votes.

distinctive voting blocs on final-passage votes. Two communities, one small and one large, emerged in the 112th Congress, in keeping with expected patterns for final passage votes. Tea Party legislators are not a defining presence in either community. As we move to the 113th Congress, the pattern shifts. Again we have two communities, but these are much more similar in size, indicating that Republicans in the House were consistently voting in two blocs on final-passage issues. Furthermore, known Tea Partiers made up more than half the membership in one of these communities (community 1), joined by a portion of aligned Republicans who, though not members of a Tea Party–affiliated caucus, were clearly acting as part of the faction. The patterns in the 114th Congress are nearly the inverse of those observed in the 112th. In the 114th, nearly all known Tea Partiers were part of the largest voting bloc, likely due to coordination efforts by the HFC, and their voting patterns were shared by a substantial portion of other Republicans as well.

The results on substantive votes are in line with the idea of a Tea Party insurgency taking over its host party, but the more difficult test comes from the remaining types of votes: procedural and substantive. These are the votes on which legislators tend to cooperate with party leadership. A Tea Party-dominated divide on these votes would thus provide strong evidence of an insurgency.

The covoting patterns on procedural issues are shown in figure 6.4. The pattern on these votes is nearly identical to the pattern for substantive votes: an absence of Tea Party–driven divisions in the 112th, an unravelling of the consensus in the 113th, and a large community dominated by Tea Partiers in the 114th.

Amendments are shown in Figure 6.5. Again, Tea Partiers did not seem to be voting differently from established Republicans in the 112th. Unlike the previous two networks, the amendment covoting network reveals the presence of a large Tea Party–dominated voting bloc beginning in the 113th and remaining relatively constant through the 114th.

The patterns in these covoting networks are certainly in line with the argument that the Tea Party represented a distinct faction in the House. Not only that, but Tea Partiers seemed to have grown increasingly unified and dominant as time went on. By the 114th Congress, Tea Party legislators had become something like the new Republican mainstream.

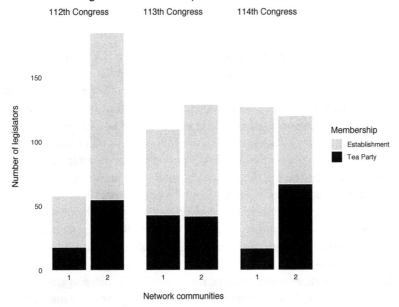

FIGURE 6.4. House Republicans increasingly shifted toward the Tea Party on procedural votes.

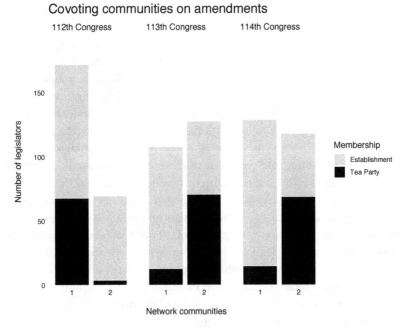

FIGURE 6.5. House Republicans increasingly shifted toward the Tea Party on amendment votes.

Cosponsoring

Legislative cosponsorships have been permitted in the US House since the 1960s. Unlike roll-call votes, which occur only at the last stage of the legislative process (once a bill has made it onto the speaker's agenda and through committee), cosponsorships occur at one of the first stages. Members cosponsor legislation long before the legislative agenda is set, meaning that party leaders do not exert influence over cosponsorships in the way they do over roll-call votes. Although cosponsorships can sometimes influence the legislative agenda, most bills never make it to the floor for consideration, regardless of who cosponsors them. Legislators frequently use cosponsorships to advertise their positions or actions on issues,[26] or to highlight their relationships with other representatives.[27]

The analysis here proceeds in a similar fashion to that used for covoting. I analyzed the 112th, 113th, and 114th Congresses as distinct networks. In each network, members were considered linked if they cosponsored the same bill. Again, I used a community detection algorithm to discover the presence of any cosponsorship blocs. Finally, I examined whether Tea Party caucus membership explains the structure of these divisions.

Figure 6.6 displays the cosponsorship communities for each of these networks. As with covoting, the 112th Congress did not feature a distinctively Tea Party cosponsorship community. Both the 113th and 114th Congresses featured three communities, all of which were largely made up of Tea Party legislators. In short, Tea Partiers engaged in substantially more cosponsorship activity than their establishment counterparts did. In addition, Tea Partiers seemed to be cosponsoring mainly with other Tea Partiers. Although this does not necessarily underscore divisions in the House, it is in line with recent findings that legislators affiliated with the Tea Party were incredibly active.[28] These analyses of patterns in the covoting and cosponsorship behavior of House Republicans in the 112th to 114th Congresses both corroborate previous findings and produce exciting new insights. The cosponsorship networks highlight Tea Partiers' tendency to cooperate with one another, and the procedural and amendment covoting networks show Tea Partiers' propensity to diverge from party leadership, in keeping with what we might expect from an insurgent faction. Perhaps most importantly, all three covoting networks underscore the evolution of the Tea Party's influence in the House, from its early days as a disorganized minority to its emergence as the leading voice in the Republican Party.

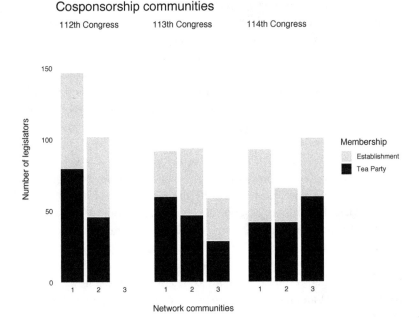

FIGURE 6.6. Patterns in the cosponsorship networks show that Tea Partiers were more active cosponsors than other Republicans.

Policy Preferences of Tea Party Legislators

Analysis of voting and cosponsorship can tell us how legislators acted, but does not tell us why. For that, I turn to press releases. Legislators traditionally use press releases to signal their policy priorities and advertise their accomplishments to constituents back in their districts.[29] The topics about which members issue releases and the language they use to discuss these topics provide insights about how legislators wish to be perceived. They can also help us answer the final question of this chapter: Were there systematic differences in how Tea Party representatives and establishment Republicans presented themselves and their priorities to the public?

I summarized the content of the 58,750 press releases issued by House Republicans between 2011 and 2015 using a structural topic model (STM). Like other topic models, STM can be used to uncover the topics discussed in a set of documents. It also facilitates the estimation of relationships between these topics and covariates of interest. It is thus uniquely suited to the task of identifying whether Tea Party representatives were more likely to discuss certain topics. I used STM to estimate the corpus as a combination of 110 distinct topics (details about preprocessing, selection of topic number, and model specification can be found in the technical appendix), and to estimate the relationship between each topic and being a Tea Partier. I controlled for the potential confounding effects of ideology (as in figure 6.2), district conservatism, and the year of release.[30]

I then classified these topics in a two-step process. First, I assigned each topic a label on the basis of the ten most distinct words in that topic. For example, a topic distinguished by the words "spending," "budget," "cuts," "deficit," "billion," "sequester," "sequestration," "fiscal," "cbo," and "reduction" received the label "budget sequestration." The budget sequestration topic was, more generally, one of many topics discussing economic and budgetary issues. In the second step, I created groupings of topics pertaining to similar issue areas, resulting in the follow seven categories: district and member information, general domestic policy, fiscal policy, Congress, interbranch relations, and discussion of conservatives.

Figure 6.7 shows the proportion of all Republican press releases that fit under each grouping. Not surprisingly, 31 percent of all press release content had something to do with members' district-centered activities, from paving roads to attending parades. The next most common issue area was *domestic policy*, comprising topics on issues like health care, abortion, and immigration (but not fiscal policy, which was its own category). Roughly 23 percent of all press release content focused on domestic policy topics. Next, 16 percent of press release content fell within the *fiscal policy* category, which was made up of topics on fiscal policy, debt, the budget, jobs, taxes, and businesses. The *Congress* category contained the 12 percent of press releases on the activities of Congress or its committees. Another 7 percent of press releases related to *foreign policy*, including topics on national defense, foreign conflicts, and allies. *Interbranch relations* followed with 6 percent of press releases, encompassing topics on the other two branches of government and their relationship with Congress. A little under 3 percent of press releases pertained to *conservative* issues, which contained a topic about the IRS's controversial scrutiny of conservative nonprofits.[31]

With this context in mind, it is time to examine whether Tea Party representatives discussed different issues in their press releases than

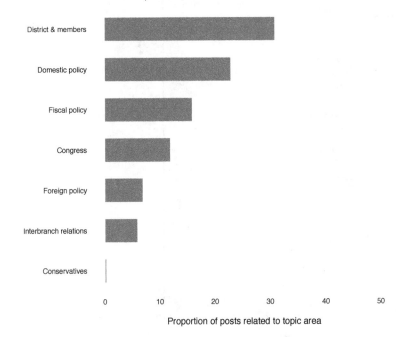

FIGURE 6.7. Summary of issue coverage in House Republicans' press releases

other Republicans did. Of the 110 topics discovered by the model, 46 were correlated with Tea Party membership. Twenty-two of these topics were positively correlated with being a Tea Partier, meaning that Tea Party affiliation made a representative *more likely* to discuss these topics. Twenty-four were negatively correlated with the Tea Party, meaning that Tea Partiers were *less likely* to talk about about these topics. Stated otherwise, topics positively correlated with the Tea Party can be thought of as *high coverage* topics, while those that were negatively correlated can be thought of as *low coverage.*

The topics correlated with Tea Party affiliation are shown in figure 6.8, along with their coefficients.[32] The topic labels used here are based on the ten most distinctive words in each topic. Coefficients on the left side of the solid vertical line indicate that Tea Partiers were less likely to discuss a certain topic, while those on the right side of the line indicate that Tea Partiers were more likely to discuss that topic. I show examples

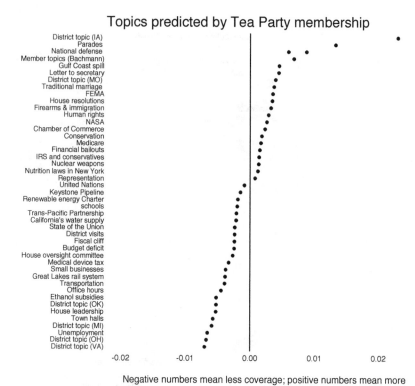

Topics predicted by Tea Party membership

Negative numbers mean less coverage; positive numbers mean more

FIGURE 6.8. Topics that Tea Partiers were significantly less or more likely to cover in their press releases. State names are abbreviated.

of these topics in figures 6.9 and 6.10, grouped by general issue area. The total number of topics in each issue area is stated in parentheses.

Figure 6.9 shows topics that were positively correlated with Tea Party affiliation. Eight of these topics were related to discussions of events or issues in Tea Party members' districts, including athletes in Steve King's Iowa district, parades, Michele Bachman, securing defense spending for a district, New York's nutrition regulations, the 2010 Gulf Coast spill, and other issues in Missouri and South Carolina. Tea Partiers were also more likely to discuss five issues related to domestic policy, the content of which is in keeping with an emphasis on status threats: the Defense of Marriage Act (DOMA), firearms as a way to confront illegal immigrants, and Medicare and Social Security, as well as a topic on the National Aeronautics and Space Administration (NASA).

In terms of foreign policy, Tea Partiers devoted coverage to foreign defense and arming the military, as well as human rights (and in particular the persecution of Christians in Sudan and China). The two topics about Congress were about representation (phrased critically) and the US Chamber of Commerce's congressional awards to pro-business members. Tea Party affiliation also correlated with two topics concerning interbranch relations—one about contacting a department secretary, and the other urging the Federal Emergency Management Agency (FEMA) to be more proactive in disaster relief. Intriguingly, Tea Party affiliation was only positively associated with one topic on economics: a discussion of the corporate bailouts following the 2008 economic crisis.

Figure 6.10 shows the topics Tea Partiers were less likely to discuss. Again, the majority of these (ten) concerned issues in districts represented by non–Tea Party Republicans, including those in California, Virginia, Ohio, Michigan, and Oklahoma. They also included general discussions about city halls, ways to visit congressional offices, transportation issues, and when members would be visiting their districts. Tea Partiers were also less likely to discuss domestic policy issues

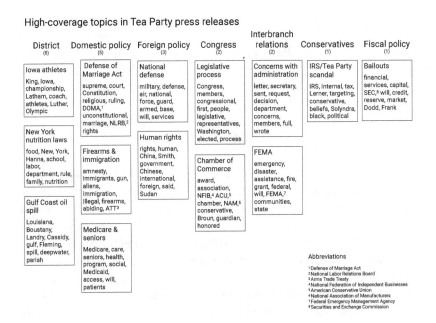

FIGURE 6.9. A closer look at the topics Tea Partiers discussed *more* in their press releases

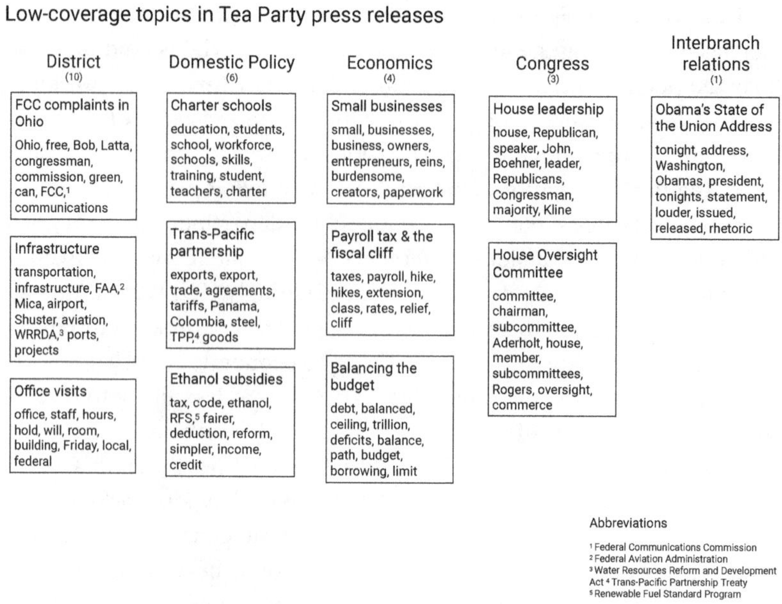

Low-coverage topics in Tea Party press releases

District (10)	Domestic Policy (6)	Economics (4)	Congress (3)	Interbranch relations (1)
FCC complaints in Ohio Ohio, free, Bob, Latta, congressman, commission, green, can, FCC,[1] communications	**Charter schools** education, students, school, workforce, schools, skills, training, student, teachers, charter	**Small businesses** small, businesses, business, owners, entrepreneurs, reins, burdensome, creators, paperwork	**House leadership** house, Republican, speaker, John, Boehner, leader, Republicans, Congressman, majority, Kline	**Obama's State of the Union Address** tonight, address, Washington, Obama, president, tonights, statement, louder, issued, released, rhetoric
Infrastructure transportation, infrastructure, FAA,[2] Mica, airport, Shuster, aviation, WRRDA,[3] ports, projects	**Trans-Pacific partnership** exports, export, trade, agreements, tariffs, Panama, Colombia, steel, TPP,[4] goods	**Payroll tax & the fiscal cliff** taxes, payroll, hike, hikes, extension, class, rates, relief, cliff	**House Oversight Committee** committee, chairman, subcommittee, Aderholt, house, member, subcommittees, Rogers, oversight, commerce	
Office visits office, staff, hours, hold, will, room, building, Friday, local, federal	**Ethanol subsidies** tax, code, ethanol, RFS,[5] fairer, deduction, reform, simpler, income, credit	**Balancing the budget** debt, balanced, ceiling, trillion, deficits, balance, path, budget, borrowing, limit		

Abbreviations

[1] Federal Communications Commission
[2] Federal Aviation Administration
[3] Water Resources Reform and Development Act [4] Trans-Pacific Partnership Treaty
[5] Renewable Fuel Standard Program

FIGURE 6.10. A closer look at the topics Tea Partiers discussed *less* in their press releases

such as ethanol subsidies, medical device taxes, the TPP trade agreement, charter schools, renewable energy, and the Keystone oil pipeline. Being part of the Tea Party negatively predicted four topics on the economy: unemployment, regulatory burdens on small businesses, balancing the budget, and concerns that the United States was approaching a "fiscal cliff" (or crisis). Tea Partiers were less likely to discuss congressional leaders, committees, and appointments. They were also less likely to discuss one topic under interbranch relations: Obama's State of the Union addresses.

Some of these findings are unsurprising. For example, Tea Partiers were more likely to discuss issues in their districts than in other districts. The more interesting findings involve which policy-related topics Tea Partiers were more and less likely to discuss. Like their activist counterparts, they were more likely to discuss preventing threats to a traditional way of life, including threats to traditional marriage (DOMA) and threats from immigrants with firearms, the IRS, and other nations. An additional set of topics reflected a suspicion of elites. For example, when Tea Partiers talked about government they did not discuss the daily process of governing, but instead expressed a general disdain for other

Republicans (criticizing the way other legislators represented their constituents), and for government agencies (chastising the IRS and FEMA). They were also less concerned with House leadership than with approval by conservative interest groups like the US Chamber of Commerce or the American Conservative Union.

Despite the movement's fiscal branding, Tea Partiers were *less* likely than their establishment counterparts to discuss economic issues. Being part of the Tea Party also meant that a legislator was less likely to discuss issues related to government regulation, such as subsidies, taxes, trade, charter schools, and the Keystone pipeline—all of which are issues that we would expect legislators focused on small government and the free market to discuss.

Summary: Connecting the Insurgency to Congress

The Tea Party had provided a unique opportunity to examine how a faction confronts its host party across different levels of government. Generally, we know more about how factions operate in national arenas like Congress and presidential nominations than we do about how they manifest in state and local contexts. This is apparent in how scholars tend to refer to the Tea Party. Although political scientists are typically careful about making distinctions and naming phenomena, those writing about the Tea Party among activists and its impact on party organization referred to it unequivocally as a "movement." Even those writing on Congress tended to distinguish between the Tea Party as a faction in Congress and its manifestation among activists, as if the two were mutually exclusive. As Rubin wrote about the HFC, ". . . the power of Republican hardliners today should not be viewed as the inevitable consequence of twenty-first century Tea Party activism." Instead, she argued, the tactical and organizational prowess of intraparty organizations in Congress spurred conservative activism: "Insurgent senators and representatives offered Republican voters angered by the political clout of eastern financiers the promise that their views would be heard in Washington."[33]

This distinction between intraparty organizations in Congress and among activists tends toward the procrustean. We know that the Republican Party's organization operates differently across national, state, and local contexts. Why, then, would we expect a Republican Party faction to operate in only one way, or in only one context?

The same insurgent tactics documented here and in other work on the Tea Party in Congress were used extensively by activists, in many cases prior to or even concurrent with similar insurgent tactics in the House. Throughout this book, I have treated the Tea Party as an example of an insurgent faction, characterized by its willingness to undermine its host party in order to gain control of it. The Tea Party in Congress was no different. Indeed, it can be viewed as a general model of how a party faction uses obstructionist strategies to undermine its host party and take it over. It is not that the Tea Party was a faction in Congress in a way that it was not among activists; it is simply that these behaviors are easier to parse at the scale of the US House.

This chapter should be read as an attempt to bridge the gap between the insurgent actions of Tea Party activists in state and local contexts and the behavior of Tea Party–affiliated legislators in Congress. Not only did Tea Partiers in the House behave differently from other Republicans, but they had different priorities as well. The priorities expressed in these press releases provide important insights into the policy agenda that drove the faction's congressional insurgency.

Of course, this leaves unaddressed many aspects of congressional parties in general, and of the Tea Party in Congress in particular. In terms of congressional parties, I have focused on broad manifestations of insurgent behavior and what motivates this behavior, with an eye to connecting these trends to the faction's behavior elsewhere. This chapter should not be read as offering a comprehensive account of party factions in the House, or as modifying or responding to a particular theory of Congress. Similarly, the focus on factional strategies as responses to different institutional incentives should not be read as a substitute for the kind of detailed account of the Tea Party's congressional presence that scholars such as Gervais and Morris offer.

In the following chapter, I will conclude by returning to questions that have lingered throughout the book: How can we understand factions apart from formal organizational mechanisms, such as congressional caucuses, especially if a faction goes by various names? How do we know when an insurgent faction, in particular, has succeeded in remaking its host party, and when that faction has simply faded away? What are the broader impacts of the Tea Party's insurgency on the Republican Party? And finally, what lessons does this theory of factions hold for American politics writ large?

CHAPTER SEVEN

Conclusion: When Factions Take Over Parties

There are two methods of curing the mischiefs of faction: the one, by removing its causes; the other, by controlling its effects. — James Madison, *Federalist* 10

The real question to ask is: what will we lose if we win? — Hannah Arendt, during a discussion of women's liberation at an *American Scholar* editorial board meeting in 1972

In the course of this research, I encountered two general perspectives on the Tea Party. The first was that the Tea Party was a political force to be reckoned with. The Tea Partiers I interviewed were hopeful that their insurgency would have lasting impacts on the Republican Party and on the nation as a whole. Political figures in the Republican and Libertarian parties acknowledged this impact. In off-the-record conversations, state-level Republican party officials recounted how the Tea Party had taken over their party. Libertarian activists and politicians discussed their initial hopes for the Tea Party, and their attendant dismay as it became apparent that the Tea Party's political mission had little to do with spreading libertarian ideals.

Not everyone took the Tea Party so seriously. Many commentators and bystanders saw it as inconsequential, even comical. This manifested in hot takes of the Tea Party as a dark-money conspiracy funded by the Koch brothers, the Christian right all over again, just racism, something not very important, a bunch of weirdos, something that would not matter in a few years, something responsible for the government shutdown, something dead, the result of economic disenfranchisement, and a stepping stone for Trump. These comments almost always came from people who had never had a conversation with a conservative, much less a Tea

Partier, but who seemed to believe that trivializing the Tea Party would neuter its influence.

Political scientists were more willing to engage in serious discussions about the Tea Party's impact on politics. Yet, even among academics, there was a tendency to treat the Tea Party as a circus curiosity. Scholars who were trained to draw fine distinctions between and within political phenomena persisted in referring to the Tea Party in the vaguest of terms, as a "movement" or an "episode." Again, it was almost as if those who found the Tea Party unsettling thought that trivializing it would make it disappear.

To be sure, the Tea Party was not always easy to take seriously. Its first widely publicized events were replete with retirement-aged Americans sporting tricorn hats and American flag regalia. It was a magnet for fringe conservative figures, like Glenn Beck and Sarah Palin. Protestors carried signs with messages ranging from the blatantly racist ("Obama bin Lyin': Impeach now!") to the Reaganesque ("My hope is in God, not govt"), to the proto-Trumpean ("Drain the swamp of socialist corruption"), to the memeworthy ("Keep your government hands off my Medicare!").[1] But while the Tea Party continued to evolve after its early protest days, general perceptions of it did not. The Tea Party's maturation into a Republican faction, and the insurgent strategies with which it continually punished its party, went largely unnoticed.

Again, it is not entirely surprising that many observers overlooked the Tea Party's factional influence. It waged its insurgency within the Republican Party, frequently at state and local levels, making it difficult to spot from the outside. What is more, the Republican Party in the era of the Tea Party seemed to be doing well. It had seized majorities in most state legislatures and in Congress. With the exception of a few high-profile incidents such as takedowns of Eric Cantor and John Boehner, the Tea Party's takeover of the Republican Party remained below most observers' political radar. This changed abruptly with the 2016 Republican nomination of Donald Trump. Trump did not have any official ties to the Tea Party—indeed, the Tea Party label was no longer part of common parlance—but the overlap between his bellicose racism and that of the Tea Party was too obvious to ignore.[2] Even so, we still possessed little in the way of an explanation for how this "movement" managed to influence US politics at such a scale.

This book offers just such an explanation, based on a simple intuition:

The Tea Party cannot be understood apart from the political institutions and systems from which it arose. It was a particular type of institutional actor (a faction) in the context of a US political institution (parties). Not only that, but the Tea Party was an *insurgent* faction—a type characterized by its ruthless strategies for remaking its host party. It developed an organizational apparatus that mirrored that of its host party in local, state, and national arenas. Using this apparatus, it contested establishment Republican candidates in nominating contests, stymied the efforts of establishment leadership in the House, and eventually forced a change in what it meant to be a conservative.

Analyzing the Tea Party in its political context allows us to explain a range of phenomena, including how it was able to reshape the Republican coalition, what similarities it bore to past factions, and whether a Tea Party can or does exist on the left. Some of these questions have been addressed in this book, but others remain unexplored. In this final chapter, I address a few lingering issues. The first two concern party factions more generally. I offer a way to identify factions within and across political institutions, and I discuss what success and failure mean for factions. I then return to the Tea Party specifically, explaining the legacy it left for the Republican Party, and whether it signals a new era of factional party politics.

Identifying Factions on the Basis of Their Behavior

Party factions are notoriously hard to identify. Aside from the occasional use of formal institutional structures such as congressional caucuses, factions do not possess clear ways in which to declare their existence or define their boundaries. These definitional ambiguities surround the Tea Party as well. Even in a limited context, such as the US House of Representatives during a six-year time period, no clear metric exists for identifying members of the Tea Party faction in Congress. If we cannot accurately identify a faction in one chamber of Congress, how can we hope to identify its presence in the messier contexts of state and local politics, or in nomination battles?

The definition of factions I have offered in this book presents an answer. A party faction is an intraparty group, distinguished from other groups in its coalition by its demands for a renegotiation of its party's consensus. Factions differ from one another in the type of renegotiation they demand (programmatic or particular) and the strategies they use to enforce their demands. Insurgent factions like the Tea Party are distinguished by their demands for partywide change, and their willingness to use combative strategies to force this change. Consociational factions, like the Christian Right, also demand partywide change, but are able to enforce these demands through more cooperative power-sharing agreements. Unlike insurgent and consociational factions, particularistic factions make demands that are limited and specific, such as the nomination of a certain candidate.

I have used the Tea Party as an illustration of an insurgent faction. Across a variety of contexts it contested the Republican Party for terrain, eventually seeking change in the form of a party takeover. As in any insurgency, the exact application of these strategies differed on the basis of the terrain in question. When presented with state Republican nominating conventions, Tea Partiers sought to "game" these conventions to the advantage of their favored candidates. In Congress, Tea Partiers obstructed and undermined their party's leadership.

This definition of factions also allows us to answer two more difficult questions about factions. Stated in terms of the Tea Party: What distinguishes members of the Tea Party as a faction from other conservative hardliners, and how can we tell if the HFC and the Tea Party activists in state and local elections are part of the same faction?

Again, we can distinguish faction members by their behavior, in recognition that an insurgent by any other name is still an insurgent. It was insurgent behavior that distinguished the Tea Party as a faction from others on the right who preferred cooperation with the Republican establishment over confrontation. In short, when a group of political actors mobilize within the same party at the same time, using insurgent strategies to make the same demands on their host party, we can consider them part of the same faction. The exact name they adopt at a given level of party organization matters very little. Legislators who used the HFC in 2015 to confront Republican leadership behaved as insurgents in line with the broader Tea Party faction, a characterization that would be true regardless of the caucus's name. Conversely, legislators who received donations from Tea Party–related PACs in 2012 but did not engage in any insurgent behavior would not be considered part of the Tea Party faction, regardless of how enthusiastically they embraced the Tea Party label.

What Factions Lose When They Win

We now turn to the question of what it means for a faction to succeed. This can be difficult to answer, largely because success and failure have similar effects on a faction: its dissolution. For most factions, success means effecting a new equilibrium in their party coalition. If we wish to understand a faction's success, we must do so on its terms. For the Tea Party, success meant wresting control of the Republican Party. Achieving this would, by extension, mean that the Tea Party would no longer have a reason to exist as an independent force.

Throughout this book, I have referred to the Tea Party using the past tense. Between 2016 and 2018, if not earlier, the Tea Party ceased to represent a distinct factional presence within the Republican Party. Although the election of a Republican president may have contributed to the Tea Party's denouement, the key element in diagnosing its demise involved its behavior toward the Republican Party. It no longer threatened establishment Republican candidates with a primary challenge from the right, and it no longer sought to undermine House leadership at all cost. Why? Because the Tea Party had more or less succeeded in eliciting its desired concessions. There were no more establishment candidates to primary; Tea Party–friendly legislators were in the plurality, if not the majority, of the Republican caucus; and a Tea Party–style candidate had prevailed in the party's presidential primary. Thus, the disappearance of the Tea Party from contemporary politics does not represent a failure—at least not if we think about what success means to a faction.

Of course, there are some who think the Tea Party was less than victorious, especially among those who still think of it as a movement dedicated to fiscal conservatism. This misconception is common enough to be worth addressing briefly here.

In February 2013 I interviewed Matt Kibbe in his FreedomWorks offices near the US Capitol in Washington. At the time, Kibbe was very much the poster child for a certain vision of the Tea Party. With a BA in economics from Grove City (a conservative Christian college), and a professional resume linking him to Republican members of Congress, the Republican National Committee, and the Koch-funded libertarian institutes at George Mason University, it was only fitting that he rose to the leadership of one of the Tea Party's most prominent umbrella organizations.

At one point in the interview, Kibbe lauded the activists whom he saw as the core of the Tea Party, calling them a "constituency for freedom that economists would've called rationally ignorant." In other words, he saw Tea Party activists as fertile soil for the libertarian message of groups like FreedomWorks, a Koch-funded group that predated the Tea Party by at least five years. Kibbe proudly detailed how "FreedomWorks organized the million-man march on Washington" by raising half a million dollars to build a stage, getting permits for portable bathrooms, and advertising the march using their Internet influence.

FreedomWorks and other libertarian groups initially invested so much time and energy in the Tea Party because they saw it as an opportunity to provide sympathetic voters with the kind of information that would allow the Koch-funded apparatus they represented to gain influence in government. By 2015, Kibbe had given up on this dream. No longer convinced that the Tea Party or the Republican Party were vehicles for his cause, he left FreedomWorks to start his own organization, Free the People, which focused on nominating third-party and libertarian candidates. What had changed for Kibbe between 2013 and 2015? The Tea Party brand had become less prominent nationally, to be sure, but it had not disappeared. The year 2015 was, after all, when the Freedom Caucus was formed and Paul Ryan became speaker of the House. The bigger change was a shift in the balance of power within the Tea Party coalition. It had grown too unwieldy for fiscally libertarian organizations like FreedomWorks to handle. They could not control its messaging, which increasingly tilted toward threat-centric rhetoric.

Fiscal conservatives and organizations like FreedomWorks were losers in the faction's development. They were not the only ones. An earlier group of Tea Party sympathizers was represented by the Tea Party caucus. These were establishment Republicans, like Michele Bachmann and Sarah Palin, who saw the Tea Party as an infusion of energy into an aging GOP. By 2015, when candidates for the Republican presidential nomination began to emerge, the real implications of the Tea Party for the GOP came into relief. While no longer relying solely on the Tea Party brand, the faction had succeeded in splintering the Republican Party, starting a tense dialogue about the very content of conservatism.

Trump and the Tea Party's Legacy

This brings us to the broader impacts of the Tea Party's insurgency on the Republican coalition. Insurgent factions behave in contestational ways toward their host parties because they want wide-scale party change. Tea Partiers' issue priorities and rhetoric, as presented here and in nearly every every major scholarly work on the Tea Party,[3] suggest that this change involved a restoration of their lost dominance, not just in the Republican coalition but in American politics and culture. Stated otherwise, the Tea Party's end goal can be understood as a renegotiation of the Republican consensus—one that elevated people and issues in line with reactionary conservatism.

Trump's candidacy and victory can be understood as symptomatic of this renegotiation. Trump's use of demeaning and bombastic rhetoric toward a variety of out-groups is not new in itself, but it is new coming from a president. More interesting still, a substantial number of voters did not find it particularly vexing. Indeed, some found it persuasive. The acceptability of Trump's reactionary rhetoric is perhaps one part of the Tea Party's legacy. After all, for more than six years preceding Trump's candidacy, reactionary conservatism had been a signature of the Tea Party, manifesting itself in activists' blog posts, in the positions of Tea Party–identifying voters, in congressional press releases and tweets, and beyond.[4] Trump did not start this shift, but he did benefit from it. By 2016, reactionary rhetoric and issue emphases were part of contemporary political conversations in a new way.

The surprise over Trump's nomination stemmed from a misunderstanding of what the Tea Party stood for and the extent of its influence over the Republican Party. If the Tea Party really had been dedicated to libertarian ideals, then a candidate like Donald Trump would have been out of the question for its activist base. But, as a faction primarily oriented toward taking over the Republican Party to preserve a way of life and wrest control from political elites, the Tea Party could have found no better candidate than Trump. Here was a figure whose brazen disregard for political correctness or decorum, derision of the political establishment, and jingoist rhetoric toward nonwhites and nonnationals fit precisely with the language activists had been using for some time in their blog posts and elsewhere.

The Tea Party had effectively removed whatever obstacles stood in the path of a candidate like Trump. It had brought a strategy of outsider opposition into the political mainstream, and established an alternative informational apparatus (from Breitbart to Americans for Prosperity, as seen in chapter 4). In addition, the Tea Party had created an environment in which contesting one's own party as an outsider was a viable way to operate politically. This legacy is not limited to the person of Trump. Of Trump's Republican competitors for the nomination in 2016, very few represented the compassionate conservatism of George W. Bush or the fusionism of Ronald Reagan. In this field, candidates who would have been considered extremist in 2000, 2008, or even 2012, such as Ted Cruz and Marco Rubio, had become viable contenders, and could even be regarded as establishment candidates.

Put otherwise, the Tea Party has shifted what it means to be conservative—not only to the right, but toward inclusion of a different set of issues consistent with the status politics of reactionary conservatism. It is not the presence of this style of conservatism on the right that is new—after all, the America Firsters, John Birch Society members, and the Goldwater wing of the Republican Party in the mid-twentieth century could be characterized in this way as well.[5] But the Tea Party has succeeded where these earlier factions have failed. It has made the status politics of reactionary conservatism part of the Republican mainstream.

Death by a Thousand Tea Parties

The Tea Party is not the first insurgent faction to establish outposts across different levels of its party, nor will it be the last. I have treated it as a member of the larger class of party factions, rather than as a political anomaly. In so doing, I have sought to draw out the features of the Tea Party that have applied and may continue to apply to other party factions in the United States. In this final section I discuss the possibility of seeing similar factions in the future—in particular, on the American left. This involves addressing two popular perspectives, both of which ignore the features that distinguish the Tea Party as a faction. The first treats the Tea Party as exclusively a creature of the right, in line with far-right populist parties and movements in Europe, and thus overplays its uniqueness. The second is exhibited in the recent tendency to cry "Tea

Party!" in response to any hint of intraparty disagreement, a perspective that underplays the Tea Party's uniqueness.

The Tea Party arose on the right just as America's first black president took office. The rhetoric and ideological priorities of its members took on an us-versus-them quality, depicting white Christian Americans as "us," and political elites, nonwhites, and nonnatives as "them." This much has been established in existing work on the Tea Party.[6] This Manichean-style distinction between "us" and "them" has a variety of manifestations, one of which is populism. Against the backdrop of discussions of far-right populist movements in Europe, some observers heralded the Tea Party as the American version of far-right populism.[7]

While the Tea Party bore ideological similarities to other far-right insurgencies, it could hardly be considered populist. In the words of Cas Mudde, a leading scholar on political extremism, populism is a "thin ideology," capable of expressing politics in only one way: as a conflict between the people and the powerful.[8] The Tea Party's reaction extended beyond "the powerful" to encompass all perceived threats to their way of life, including those from cultural outsiders. Tea Partiers' use of populist rhetoric (e.g., "Drain the swamp") was belied by their behavior as a faction. They did not follow a charismatic leader in order to rise up against the corrupt ruling class. Rather, they used combative strategies to elevate themselves to positions in that ruling class.

If we wish to draw lessons from the Tea Party for other factional episodes in the United States, we must distinguish between its ideological program and the institutional mechanisms it used to force its host party to adopt that program. Most fundamentally, a faction can be understood as a means of expressing political dissent in a two-party electoral system. The two major parties in such a system are coalitions of groups that agree to compromise on a shared agenda. These compromises will inevitably benefit some groups more than others, and some groups not at all. The neglected groups have very few options for recourse. Although such a group might mobilize as a minor party in another electoral system, it will find gaining access to the ballot as a third party in the United States to be exceedingly difficult; and even if it does accomplish that, the strategy rarely yields success. In the United States, neglected groups can wait for their fortunes to turn; or, if they can form a coalition with other neglected groups, they can form a faction.

A faction is a subcoalition of groups that agree to work together to

increase their influence in their party coalition. Factions can avail themselves of different strategies in this quest for influence, on the basis of
factors including strengths and weaknesses in the party's organizational
makeup, nominating institutions, or electoral base, as well as the extent
of the faction's organizational savvy, electoral reach, or activist base. In
this book I have focused on one type of faction: the insurgent faction.
An insurgent faction is distinguished by its confrontational strategies,
which manifest in a willingness to undermine its host party in order to
gain prominence in that party's coalition. The Tea Party is neither the
first nor the only party faction to use insurgent tactics. The Dixiecrats
and Goldwater's New Right, for example, were willing to undermine
their parties in order to remake them. Pending a major change in the US
electoral system, such factions are likely to arise periodically within either party whenever a group seeks more concessions than its party coalition is willing or able to grant.

Since the 2016 election, political commentators have heralded any
whiff of activism (e.g., the 2017 Women's March) or dissent (e.g., Keith
Ellison's 2017 DNC chair bid) within the Democratic Party as the "Tea
Party on the left!" What exactly commentators mean by "Tea Party on
the left" is, however, unclear. At times the phrase seems to imply that
the Tea Party represented a novel way of expressing political dissent. At
others, it functions as a catchall term for political dissatisfaction. Neither
usage is particularly conducive to identifying a Tea Party on the left, if
one indeed exists. After all, every burst of political energy is not a faction, and all factions are not the same.

The framework of factions presented in this book provides a way to
distinguish among various forms of subparty and intraparty dissent. A
Tea Party on the left would be more accurately described as an insurgent
faction in the Democratic Party. Such a faction would be distinguished
by its demands for partywide programmatic change, and its use of contestational strategies to enforce its demands. Indeed, the Democratic
Party has long been home to a progressive faction, and is, of the two major parties, the preferred vehicle of leftist or socialist candidates. Until
recently, this faction seemed to be operating in a consociational manner,
accepting policy concessions in exchange for the use of the Democratic
Party's reputation and apparatus.

Something shifted in 2016, when Bernie Sanders, a self-described
democratic socialist, contested the Democratic establishment's favored
candidate for presidential nomination.[9] Two years later, this insurgent

primary tactic emerged again in a few high-profile congressional races—such as the one in New York's 14th congressional district, where Alexandria Ocasio-Cortez, also a democratic socialist, defeated the Democratic incumbent in the primary,[10] and the one in Illinois's 3rd district, where the progressive Democrat Marie Newman unsuccessfully challenged the conservative Democratic incumbent Dan Lipinski.[11] These episodes, among others, certainly fit with what we would expect from an insurgent faction. It is indeed possible that the democratic socialists could become increasingly hostile, waging an insurgency that destabilizes the Democratic Party in the same way the Tea Party destabilized the Republican Party. So far, progressive Democrats tend to operate, as they have since the days of George McGovern, as friendly associates within the Democratic Party, occasionally pushing the party to correct course in a more progressive direction,[12] while the more doctrinaire democratic socialists continue to debate, as they have since the 1960s (then manifesting as Students for a Democratic Society and the Americans for Democratic Action), whether they should engage with the Democratic Party at all.[13]

The possibility of a Tea Party on the left illustrates a few important points about insurgent factions. First, mobilization as an insurgent faction is not a *necessary consequence* of partisan discontent. The democratic socialists and progressives could very well join together and form an insurgent faction, but this does not mean that they will. Such mobilization would require a commitment to working within the Democratic Party on the part of democratic socialists, as well as the formation of a rift between progressive Democrats and the party. The latter could be unlikely, given that the Democratic Party is historically more accommodating of different ideological styles, and thus better equipped to absorb demands for change.[14] Whether a group mobilizes as an insurgent faction, then, is dependent on at least two things: the groups within a would-be faction agreeing among themselves on their strategy and their demands, and the host party failing to accommodate those demands.

Similarly, what it means for an insurgency to be successful will vary across parties and eras. Some insurgencies may affect party realignments, others renegotiation of their coalitions, and still others minor ideological concessions. Both successful and unsuccessful factions usually end up being absorbed by a major party, their distinct identity fading, as did that of the Tea Party. Yet fading is not the same as failing.

In the end, this exploration of the Tea Party's impact on the Republican coalition can help us put US party coalitions—and the groups that make them up—in perspective. Parties are often the recipients of all manners of abuse. We blame them for any political outcome we dislike, from polarization to unpopular candidates to congressional gridlock. Embedded in these accusations are two assumptions: a belief that the parties are too powerful, and a belief that these powerful parties are responsible for the country's political discord.

If nothing else, the Tea Party's insurgency challenged these assumptions. It exposed fault lines within its party, exacerbated the conflict between the two parties, and made us more aware of potential fractures within the Democratic Party as well. The Tea Party reminded us that US parties do not speak with single voices. They are coalitions of groups that do not necessarily get along. What is more, the Tea Party called our attention to the decentralized nature of party power, which resides with myriad state and local party organizations rather than with the national party committees. In this light, the fact that the parties are stable at all is somewhat remarkable.

It is all too easy to dwell on the damage the Tea Party's insurgency left in its wake. But I would like to end this book on two more hopeful notes. First, the Tea Party's activist insurgency, and specifically its use of state and local organizations to influence party politics, signals that both civic participation and local parties are alive and well. Second, the Tea Party should leave us with a renewed appreciation of political parties and their role in muting the effects of fractious groups. As James Madison wrote so long ago, the impulse to divide into factions seems to be "sown in the nature of man." Yet insurgent factions like the Tea Party are notable *because* they arise so infrequently in the US party system. No institution, however well crafted, can root out all harmful divisions. But US parties, in bringing together diverse groups and forcing compromises, deserve some appreciation for the role they play in ameliorating the mischiefs of faction.

Technical Appendixes

Appendix to Chapter 1

Ohio

Ohio also faced Tea Party challenges in its 2010 statewide elections. Of the seventeen seats that were up for reelection in the Ohio State Senate in 2010, Libertarian candidates contested Republicans in three districts, and Republicans faced contested primaries in four districts. All ninety-nine Ohio State House seats were up for reelection in 2010. Twenty-seven of these faced challenges from Libertarian or Constitution Party candidates, and twenty-three had contested Republican primaries.[1]

Tea Partiers in Ohio ran for office as minor party candidates more frequently than Tea Partiers in Virginia did, for two reasons. First, in 2010 Ohio had electoral laws that allowed third-party candidates to access ballots easily. Second, Ohio imposes term limits on state legislators in both chambers. In practice, this means that nearly all of its contested Republican primaries in 2010 for statewide elections were in districts where the incumbents were retiring due to term limits, and were races among traditional Republican candidates. In 2010 most of these Republican incumbents did not face primary challenges from the Tea Party. Only one of the four State Senate districts with a contested Republican primary had an incumbent running, and only seven of the twenty-three State House districts with contested Republican primaries had incumbents running. Rather, Tea Partiers challenged Ohio Republicans for statewide offices in the 2010 general election, running as Libertarians.

Virginia

The circumstances confronting the Tea Party in Virginia differed from those in Ohio in several ways. Virginia had stricter state laws regulating independent parties, held its statewide elections in odd-numbered years, and did not consistently use primaries to select candidates in statewide elections. Because Virginia does not allow voters to register for a party, its state parties cannot guarantee that only their partisans vote in their primaries. Thus, many candidates for its state legislature are selected using local or county conventions. For statewide offices the RPV selects its candidates using nominating conventions, with rare exceptions.[2]

These features resulted in a radically different strategy for the Tea Party in Virginia. Things came to a head by the 2013 statewide election cycle, when the Tea Party in Virginia set its sights on that year's RPV nominating convention. The RPV's nominating conventions function on a ballot system. If no candidate for a particular statewide office wins a majority of votes on the first ballot, balloting continues. Months before the 2013 RPV nominating convention, Virginia Tea Parties began planning to fill one-third of delegate slots with Tea Partiers, and ran training sessions on the balloting process for their members. When the convention came around, Tea Partiers populated enough of the delegates to prevent other Republicans from gaining a majority on initial ballots. Unlike many other delegates, Tea Partiers stayed until 10 p.m, when, after eight rounds of balloting, their favored candidates received the RPV's nominations.

Appendix to Chapter 4

Data Collection

Data collection for this chapter took place between May 2013 and May 2014. Creating the list of Tea Party groups was a multistep process. A variety of Tea Party–related sites (e.g., Tea Party Patriots, Freedom-Works, Tea Party 9/11, and TeaParty.org) maintained lists of Tea Party groups by state and locality. I combined these lists to create a base list of Tea Party groups. I then verified that each of these groups had an active web page. In the process, I added any additional Tea Party groups linked to on these web pages. Finally, I searched the Internet for "Tea Party + [state name]," adding any additional groups returned by the search results to the list. I had three undergraduate research assistants perform similar searches, stopping only when the searches no longer yielded unique results. Finally, I unduplicated the list and standardized the group name of any local Tea Party that appeared on it multiple times under slightly variant names. This list yielded more than a thousand Tea Party groups.

To construct the Tea Party website network, I omitted any groups that did not have a semipermanent repository of links to external groups on their websites. This included Tea Party groups that only used Twitter, Facebook, password-protected Ning sites, or Meetup sites. Of the original thousand, 665 local Tea Party groups linked to external websites and were included in the network data set. In the second stage of data collection, I scraped information about any link posted on one of the Tea Party websites. Most of the sites contained clear sections labeled "Resources," "Blogroll," "Further Reading," "Like-Minded Groups," and so on. Less sophisticated Tea Party sites only had home pages, so I scraped any links from those pages as well. Once this information was collected, I unduplicated and standardized the spelling of these other websites. This produced the final set of 5,521 unique websites.

Tea Party Website Network Analysis

I transformed this list of Tea Party groups and other websites into an edge list, then used the igraph package in R to produce a directed graph (Tea Party groups linking to other websites). Table 4.a1 gives descriptive statistics for the network. Because my analysis relied on measures of centrality and community detection, I address those in greater detail below.

I used the centrality measure "in-degree" to generate the list of top-

TABLE 4.A1. **Tea Party blog network**

Attribute	Statistics
Unique organizations	665
Unique resources	5,521
Degree max	280
In-degree max	237
Density	0.00036
Modularity	0.4503
Number of communities	272
Number of isolate communities	2

linked websites (e.g., most central nodes) in this chapter. In-degree statistics are computed by counting the number of links received by a given node. If a node has a high in-degree score, this means that it received a large number of links. In the Tea Party network, an organization's in-degree score is equal to the number of Tea Party groups that linked to that organization. The maximum in-degree score in this network is 237, meaning that one organization (the Tea Party Patriots), was linked to be 237 Tea Party groups. Because this is a directed network, the same nodes are the most central using both degree and in-degree measures. Other centrality measures (betweenness, etc.) also yield a list of the same central nodes.

Figure 4.a1 shows that the majority of Tea Party groups sent and received very few links—fewer than four. The gap between the most-linked (237) and the average-linked (< 4) organizations in the network signals that (1) the network is not very dense, and (2) the organizations with high

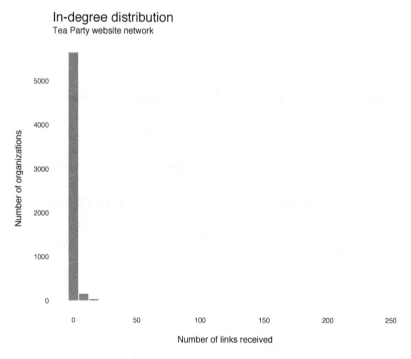

FIGURE 4.A1. Outside the top-linked websites (shown in figure 4.3), most websites in the Tea Party network were only linked to by one to four Tea Party groups.

in-degree scores provide important insight about information flows in the overall network.

The network's modularity score is also worth noting. The modularity statistic can take on values from zero to one. A score of zero indicates that no divisions exist in the network, meaning that all nodes are part of the same module. A score of one would mean that the network is completely modular, so that each node would be its own module. The extremes of zero and one are almost never observed in reality, as most networks are neither completely nonmodular nor completely modular. The modularity statistic here is 0.45. This means that 45 percent of nodes do not share connections, and 55 percent do. Because divisions are responsible for about half of the network's structure, they warrant further investigation, also known as community detection.

After experimenting with various communities detection algorithms in the igraph package in R ("fast greedy," "edge-betweenness," etc.), I report results obtained using the walktrap algorithm. Because of the size of the network, algorithms reached a resolution limit. Of the less memory-intensive algorithms, "walk trap" is one of the best at discovering small communities within a network, which it detects through a process of random walks throughout the subgraphs in a network.[3] In order to validate the results of the walktrap algorithm, I also performed community detection on a bipartite projection of the network, which yielded similar patterns.

Appendix to Chapter 5

Obtaining Data

The list of Tea Party websites analyzed in this chapter is an extended version of that used in chapter 4. The number of groups that at least posted mission statements on their web pages (1,051) exceeded both those that linked to external websites (665) and those that had blogs separate from social media feeds (200). All mission statements were included in the mission statement analysis.

The blog post analysis only included websites with blogs that were not social media feeds. Social media feeds were excluded because few groups used either Twitter or Facebook to post anything more than meeting times and memes. For those groups whose websites included blogs, I wrote custom html-based scrapers to extract and save their posts, which

I then converted to .txt files. This resulted in some 42,479 blog posts. In some cases, downloaded posts only contained captions for videos or broken links. These were removed during the preprocessing of the corpus.

Mission Statement Coding

Mission statements were coded with the help of three undergraduate research assistants. For every mission statement, research assistants were instructed to record a 1 for any of the issue priorities mentioned. Each mission statement was coded separately by two researchers to ensure accuracy. If the researchers disagreed on the coding, I performed an additional review of the mission statement.

Topic Modeling / LDA

I used a relatively standard set of preprocessing techniques, implemented through the topicmodels package in R (also used for LDA). These included the removal of symbols, punctuation, white space, numbers, and English stop words. Due to the many errors in wording and usage that appeared in these posts, I also reduced words to their common English stems. Finally, due to the recurring presence of some html strings in the extracted posts, as well as boilerplate language, I removed words that occurred in fewer than 5 percent or more than 90 percent of the posts. Any posts that at this stage no longer contained content were dropped from the resulting document-term matrix. The final document-term matrix contained 42,019 documents and 696 terms.[4]

I used a latent dirichlet allocation (LDA) model to analyze these documents.[5] Running LDA on such a large matrix required the use of high-performance computing resources. I am deeply grateful to Dr. Jens Mueller at Miami University for his assistance in gaining access to adequate resources at the Ohio Supercomputing Center. This allowed me not only to run the final model, but to test different specifications for k (the number of topics). We ran the model four times, at k's of 25, 50, 75, and 100. The final version of the model specified a k of 100. Although the topics and content from this version of the model did not differ substantially from those derived at $k = 75$, setting the topics to 100 provided the nuanced topics necessary for this analysis, as well as pulling any leftover noise (boilerplate language, html output, etc.) into separate topics, which I could separate from the substantive topics used in the analysis.[6]

Appendix to Chapter 6

Tea Partiers in Congress

Table 6.a1 lists the number of legislators in the 112th, 113th, and 114th Congresses who were members of at least one Tea Party caucus, and shows the overlap between caucus memberships. I also used community detection to discover divisions within the full voting networks (i.e., those not parsed out by type of vote). Figure 6.a1 summarizes these communities, which are a more muted version of those discovered in the vote-type networks.

STM Model

To prepare the press releases for analysis, I performed a series of pre-processing steps similar to those used in the content analysis in chap-

TABLE 6.A1. **Tea Party caucus membership**

112th Congress: 73 total			
	Freedom Caucus	Liberty Caucus	Tea Party caucus
Caucus total	26	29	54
Freedom overlap	26	17	16
Liberty overlap	17	29	13
Tea Party overlap	16	13	54

113th Congress: 85 total			
	Freedom Caucus	Liberty Caucus	Tea Party caucus
Caucus total	36	43	53
Freedom overlap	36	26	16
Liberty overlap	26	43	16
Tea Party overlap	16	16	53

114th Congress: 84 total			
	Freedom Caucus	Liberty Caucus	Tea Party caucus
Caucus total	41	39	48
Freedom overlap	41	25	15
Liberty overlap	25	39	15
Tea Party overlap	15	15	48

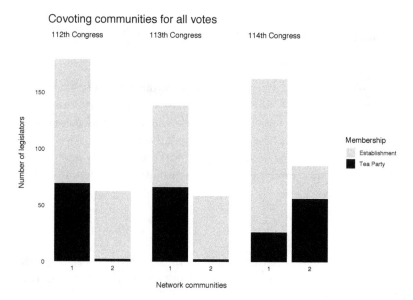

FIGURE 6.A1. House Republicans' shift towards the Tea Party is even apparent in analysis of the full covoting networks (combining final passage, procedural, and amendment votes).

ter 5. These included the removal of white space, numbers, characters, stop words, punctuation, and words that occurred in only one document. I ran the model on both a stemmed and an unstemmed version of the corpus. Both versions contained a total of 58,750 press releases. The unstemmed corpus contained 35,735 unique words, and the stemmed contained 24,107. After comparing the output and its substantive interpretation, I chose to proceed with the unstemmed corpus, which yielded more substantively meaningful topics.

STM has a built-in function (searchK) for determining the optimal k, or number of topics one asks the model to discover. I iterated over my corpus twice, first with a k ranging from 50 to 200 by intervals of 10. Based on these results, I iterated over the corpus again, this time with a k ranging from 100 to 120 by intervals of 5. The diagnostic plot is shown in figure 6.a2. On the basis of these diagnostics, 110 and 115 looked like the best options for k. I ran both models. The additional five topics with $k = 115$ were nonsense / web code topics, so I went forward with the results from $k = 110$.

I also coded and included four covariates to make use of the correlative abilities of the partially collapsed variational expectation-

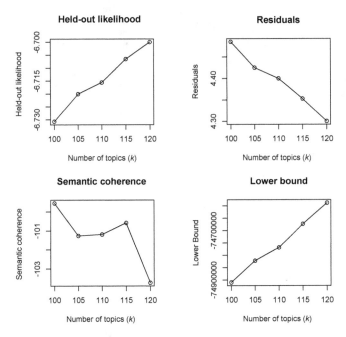

FIGURE 6.A2. These diagnostic plots suggest that a good number of topics would be between 110 and 120. Topic numbers above 110 yielded multiple "nonsense" topics characterized by .html markup or boilerplate contact language, so I performed the final analysis on $k = 110$.

maximization algorithm used by STM. Because my substantive question was whether being part of the Tea Party predicted talking more or less about a certain topic when controlling for these factors, I did not report the coefficients for any variable except Tea Party membership.

1. Tea Party membership: This was the key explanatory variable. It was coded as 1 for any member who had been part of the Tea Party, Liberty Caucus, or Freedom Caucus, and as 0 for any member who had not. I also ran a specification of the model that included separate dummy variables for membership in each of the caucuses (rather than collapsing them into one variable), but the differences among caucses were so muted that I chose to use the combined Tea Party variable in the final model.

2. Ideology: To capture relative ideological extremism, I included the DW-Nominate first dimension scores for all members.

3. District conservatism: I also included Cook's partisan voting index (PVI) for the 2012 election as a measure of how conservative or liberal the legislators' districts were during the period analyzed.

4. Year: I included a variable for year to control for the possibility correlation of certain topics with certain years.

Acknowledgments

I encountered many obstacles while working on this project, as any re-searcher does. I also encountered many people who at critical junc-tures helped me remove or navigate around those obstacles, and to whom I am deeply grateful. Hans Noel, Daniel Hopkins, Jonathan Ladd, and Clyde Wilcox have been my chief advocates and mentors. Their meth-odological and theoretical insights are reflected throughout this book. To Hans, in particular: Thank you for encouraging me to pursue diffi-cult questions, and for pushing me to rigorously answer those questions.

While in Washington, I benefited from the input and support of sev-eral individuals at Georgetown University, including Michael Bailey, Boris Shor, Mark Rom, Charles King, Gerald Mara, Richard Boyd, Douglas Reed, Diana Kapisciewski, and Alexander Podkul. I must also extend my thanks to Mark Mitchell and Frank Guliuzza from Patrick Henry College. Thank you for supporting me in the path I chose.

The many data sets and empirical analyses in this book would not have been possible without help and advice from Solomon Messing, Justin Grimmer, Michael Heaney, Matt Denny, and Jake Russ. In addition, Jens Mueller and Greg Reece of Miami University's Research Computing Sup-port Center facilitated my use of high-performance computing services.

I am grateful to the individuals who have read and offered feedback on draft chapters of this book, including Greg Koger, Daniel DiSalvo, Heath Brown, Kevin Reuning, Connor Ewing, Bryan Marshall, Seth Masket, Monica Schneider, Cailin Crockett, Megan Laws, Rebecca Merkley, Chris Collins, Jenna Lorence, Gabrielle Hesslau, and my un-dergraduate research assistants Mary Bush and Ryan Vierhile.

I owe special thanks to Christopher Parker, who once told me that a theory is a beautiful thing, and who has continually encouraged me to be bold. Paul Kellstedt has been unflagglingly generous in his feedback and support; thank you. In addition, I have been the fortunate recipient of friendship and mentorship from several women whose lives and scholarship continue to inspire me: Jennifer Victor, Marjorie Hershey, Christina Wolbrecht, Kristin Kanthak, Alison Craig, Julia Azari, and Kelsey Shoub.

I am deeply appreciative of the comments I have received on this research at conferences and talks. I am grateful to the various undergraduate research assistants who helped me with initial coding and data collection, both at Georgetown University and at Miami University. Thank you as well to the writers at the blog Mischiefs of Faction for providing me a platform on which to share early insights from this book. And thank you to my colleagues and students at Miami University.

None of this would have been possible without Chuck Myers's continued interest in the project, and guidance in moving it forward. Thank you, and thanks to the others at the University of Chicago Press, in particular Alicia Sparrow and Renaldo Migaldi. Finally, I thank my two reviewers, whose insightful comments have made this an inestimably better book.

I received kindness, generosity, and support from a number of Tea Party activists and leaders in the course of this research. To those of you who agreed to interviews, allowed me to observe and participate in their events, vouched for me to other activists and leaders, answered my surveys, and gave guest lectures in my courses: Thank you. I have attempted to respect your confidence by recounting our conversations as fairly and clearly as possible. It is my sincere hope that this book gives your activism the serious consideration it deserves. I must also extend my thanks to officials in the Republican and Libertarian Parties who spoke with me off the record, providing invaluable context for this book.

The sport of Brazilian jiu jitsu has helped me work through innumerable cases of writer's block. I am grateful to the coaches and teammates who have supported me in ways big and small. Cailin Crockett, Emily Braid, Karen Anderson, and Zoe Bridges have kept me grounded, given me shoulders to cry on, and shared my joys. My parents' confidence in my ability to both persevere and overcome has motivated me through many rough spots, both in this project and in life. My husband, Chris Collins, has been my rock in the final stages of this process: reading through drafts, talking through ideas, and protecting my time. Most of all, I am grateful for the love and support of my sister, Marla Blum, who has always there to remind me that Blums don't quit. I carry your heart with me.

Notes

Chapter One

1. These were Bishop E. W. Jackson for lieutenant governor, Mark Obenshain for attorney general, and Ken Cuccinelli for governor. Cuccinelli was the de facto nominee, as his only Republican opponent, Bill Bolling, had withdrawn from the race several months earlier.

2. Earlier that year the VATPP had prevailed in a debate about whether to switch the RPV's nominating system from conventions to primaries—a move intended to prevent the Tea Party from doing exactly what they did in 2013.

3. Laura Vozzella, "Virginia GOP Picks Staunch Conservatives as Statewide Candidates," *Washington Post*, May 19, 2013, https://www.washingtonpost.com/local/va-politics/virginiagop-picks-staunch-conservatives-a%202013/05/18/138040b4-bef7-11e2-89c9-3be8095fe767_story.html?utm_term=.6c3581e50209.

4. Bill Bartel, "Jackson Is Disappointed Rigell Won't Endorse Him," *Virginian-Pilot*, June 6, 2013, https://pilotonline.com/news/government/politics/article_9219c57d-0d3d-572fb3b0-cd791c0783f5.%20html.

5. Vanessa Williamson and Theda Skocpol, *The Tea Party and the Remaking of Republican Conservatism, Revised Ed* (New York: Oxford University Press, 2016); Christopher S. Parker and Matt A. Barreto, *Change They Can't Believe In: The Tea Party and Reactionary Politics in America* (Princeton, NJ: Princeton University Press, 2013); Bryan Gervais and Irwin Morris, *Reactionary Republicanism: How the Tea Party in the House Paved the Way for Trump's Victory* (New York: Oxford University Press, 2018).

6. Alan I. Abramowitz and Kyle L. Saunders, "Ideological Realignment in the US Electorate," *Journal of Politics* 60, no. 3 (1998): 634–52; Greg D. Adams, "Abortion: Evidence of an Issue Evolution," *American Journal of Political Science* (1997): 718–37; John H. Aldrich, *Why Parties? The Origin and Transformation of Political Parties in America* (Chicago: University of Chicago Press, 1995); Edward G. Carmines and James A Stimson, *Issue Evolution* (Princeton,

NJ: Princeton University Press, 1989); Geoffrey Layman, *The Great Divide: Religious and Cultural Conflict in American Party Politics* (New York: Columbia University Press, 2001); Nolan M. McCarty, Keith T. Poole, and Howard Rosenthal, *Income Redistribution and the Realignment of American Politics* (Washington: AEI Press, 1997); Hans Noel, *Political Ideologies and Political Parties in America* (New York: Cambridge University Press, 2013); David W. Rohde, *Parties and Leaders in the Postreform House* (Chicago: University of Chicago Press, 1991).

7. Virginia Department of Elections, "Political Party Committees," 2018, accessed March 15, 2018, at https://www.elections.virginia.gov/candidatepac-info/political-committees/political-party-committees/.

8. Ballotpedia, "Ballot Access Requirements for Political Parties in Ohio," accessed March 15, 2019, at https://ballotpedia.org/Ballot_access_requirements_for_political_parties_in_Ohio.

9. Libertarian Party, "Ohio Libertarians Get Coverage by Fielding Candidates," February 22, 2010; accessed March 15, 2019, at https://www.lp.org/blogs-staff-ohio-libertarians-get-coverage-by-fielding-candidates/.

10. A more detailed explanation of the electoral laws in both states can be found in the appendix to this chapter.

11. Open Secrets, "Ohio Congressional Races 2010," accessed April 10, 2018, at https://www.opensecrets.org/races/%20election?cycle=2010&id=KS04&state=OH.

12. Open Secrets, "Virginia Congressional Races 2010," accessed April 10, 2018, at https://www.opensecrets.%20org/races/election?cycle=2010&id=AK&state=VA. It should be noted that, despite its name, Virginia's "Independent Green Party" is an affiliate of the Independence Party of America, not the Green Party of the United States.

13. Virginia Conservative Blog, "The Rise of the LPVA," June 19, 2014, accessed April 10, 2018, at http://virginiaconservative.net/tag/stuart-bain.

14. Julie Carr Smyth, "Federal Judge Upholds Third-Party Ballot Rules in Ohio," *Akron Beacon Journal*, April 16, 2015, accessed April 10, 2018, at https://www.ohio.com/akron/news/federaljudge-upholds-third-party-ballot-rules-in-ohio.

15. Henry J Gomez, "Portage County Tea Party Leader Tom Zawistowski Launches Bid to Be Next Ohio GOP Chairman," Cleveland.com, April 2, 2013; accessed April 10, 2018, at http://www.cleveland.com/open/index.ssf/2013/04/%20portage_county_tea_party_leade.html.

16. Brian Stelter, "CNBC Replays Its Reporter's Tirade," *New York Times,* February 22, 2009, accessed July 30, 2019, at https://www.nytimes.com/2009/02/23/business/media/23cnbc.html.

17. Dick Armey and Matt Kibbe, *Give Us Liberty: A Tea Party Manifesto* (New York City: William Morrow, 2011); Heath Brown, *The Tea Party*

Divided: The Hidden Diversity of a Maturing Movement (Santa Barbara, CA: ABC-CLIO, 2015).

18. Burghart, "View from the Top: Reports on Six National Tea Party Organizations"; Lo, "Astroturf versus Grass Roots: Scenes from Early Tea Party Mobilization"; Zernike, *Boiling Mad: Inside Tea Party America.*

19. Zachary Courser, "The Tea Party at the Election," *The Forum* 8, no. 4 (June 2011).

20. David T. Canon, "The Year of the Outsider: Political Amateurs in the US Congress," *The Forum* 8, no. 4 (January 2011).

21. Michael Bailey, Jonathan Mummolo, and Hans Noel, "The Tea Party and Congressional Representation: Tracking the Influence of Activists, Groups and Elites," *American Politics Research* 20, no. 10 (2012): 1–3; Gary C. Jacobson, "The President, the Tea Party, and Voting Behavior in 2010: Insights from the Cooperative Congressional Election Study," *APSA 2011 Annual Meeting Paper*, August 2011.

22. Steven Shepard, "Poll: Majority of Voters Back Trump Travel Ban," *Politico*, July 5, 2017, accessed March 10, 2019, at https://www.politico.com/story/2017/07/05/trump-travel-ban-poll-voters-240215; Aaron Blake, "Whip Count: Here's Where Republicans Stand on Trump's Controversial Travel Ban," *Washington Post*, January 29, 2017; accessed April 10, 2018, at https://www.washingtonpost.com/news/the-fix/wp/2017/01/29/heres-where-republicans-stand-on-president-t%20?utm_term=.a4bf0681f98e.

23. David Hume, "Of the Coalition of Parties," in *On the Side of the Angels: An Appreciation of Parties and Partisanship*, ed. Nancy L Rosenblum (Princeton, NJ: Princeton University Press, 2008), 122.

24. David R. Mayhew, *Placing Parties in American Politics: Organization, Electoral Settings, and Government Activity in the Twentieth Century* (Princeton, NJ: Princeton University Press, 1986).

25. Giovanni Sartori, *Parties and Party Systems: A Framework for Analysis* (New York: Cambridge University Press, 1976).

26. Daniel DiSalvo, *Engines of Change: Party Factions in American Politics, 1868–2010* (New York: Oxford University Press, 2012).

27. Interest groups, pressure groups, and social and political movements are referred to in a variety of ways by different scholars. This book does not take a position on the finer points of these debates. Throughout, I use the terms "interest groups" and "movements" or "social movements" for consistency and clarity.

28. Jacob Hamilton, "Bernie Sanders Faces Two Big Challenges as He Enters the 2020 Race," NBC News, February 19, 2019; accessed March 18, 2019, at https://www.nbcnews.com/politics/meet-the-press/bernie-sanders-faces-two-big-challenges-he-enters-2020-race-n973006.

29. Parker and Barreto, *Change They Can't Believe In*; Gervais and Morris, *Reactionary Republicanism*; Brenda Major, Alison Blodorn, and Gregory Major

Blascovich, "The Threat of Increasing Diversity: Why Many White Americans Support Trump in the 2016 Presidential Election," *Group Processes and Intergroup Relations* 21, no. 6 (2018): 931–40.

Chapter Two

1. DiSalvo, *Engines of Change*, xii.

2. Nancy L. Rosenblum, *On the Side of the Angels: An Appreciation of Parties and Partisanship* (Princeton, NJ: Princeton University Press, 2008), 2.

3. Schattschneider, *Party Government*.

4. For example, V. O. Key, *Politics, Parties, and Pressure Groups*, 4th edition, (Thomas Y. Crowell, 1958); Russell J. Dalton, David M. Farrell, and Ian McAllister, *Political Parties and Democratic Linkage: How Parties Organize Democracy* (New York: Oxford University Press, 2011); Robert Alan Dahl, *Dilemmas of Pluralist Democracy: Autonomy vs. Control* (New Haven: Yale University Press, 1982); Susan C. Stokes, "Political Parties and Democracy," *Annual Review of Political Science* 2, no. 1 (1999): 243–67. All see parties as inevitable in democracy, but their different definitions of parties impact their evaluations of the relationship between parties and representation.

5. Noel, *Political Ideologies and Political Parties in America*; Matthew Levendusky, *The Partisan Sort: How Liberals Became Democrats and Conservatives Became Republicans* (Chicago: University of Chicago Press, 2009).

6. See Alan I. Abramowitz, *The Disappearing Center: Engaged Citizens, Polarization, and American Democracy* (New Haven: Yale University Press, 2010); Abramowitz and Saunders, "Ideological Realignment in the US Electorate"; Marc J. Hetherington, "Resurgent Mass Partisanship: The Role of Elite Polarization," *American Political Science Review* 95, no. 3 (2001): 619–31; Gary C. Jacobson, "Party Polarization in National Politics: The Electoral Connection," in *Polarized Politics: Congress and the President in a Partisan Era*, vol. 5, ed. Jon Bond and Richard Fleisher (Washington: CQ Press, 2000), 17–18; Lilliana Mason, "'I Disrespectfully Agree': The Differential Effects of Partisan Sorting on Social and Issue Polarization," *American Political Science Review* 59, no. 1 (2015): 128–45; Keith T. Poole and Howard Rosenthal, "The Polarization of American Politics," *Journal of Politics* 46, no. 4 (1984): 1061–79; Barbara Sinclair, *Party Wars: Polarization and the Politics of National Policy Making* (Norman: University of Oklahoma Press, 2014); and Sean M. Theriault, *Party Polarization in Congress* (Cambridge: Cambridge University Press, 2008), among others.

7. Carl Bilaik, "How the Republican Field Dwindled from 17 to Donald Trump," FiveThirtyEight, May 5, 2016; accessed August 9, 2019, at https://

fivethirtyeight.com/features/how-the-republican-field-dwindled-from-17-to
-donald-trump/.

8. Philip Bump, "The 2016 GOP Presidential Race, Broken Down into 5 'Lanes,'" *Washington Post*, March 25, 2015; accessed August 9, 2019, at https://www.washingtonpost.com/news/the-fix/wp/2015/03/25/breaking-down-the-lanes-theory-of-the-2016-republican-field/?utm_term=.8a6665fcc54f.

9. Douglass Adair, *Fame and the Founding Fathers: Essays by Douglass Adair*, ed. Trevor Coulbourn (Indianapolis: Liberty Fund, 1998); Theodore Draper, "Hume and Madison: The Secrets of Federalist Paper no. 10," *Encounter* 58, no. 34 (1982); Henry Farnham May, *The Enlightenment in America* (New York: Oxford University Press, 1976).

10. Hume, *History of England*, 3:19–20.

11. Note the interchangeable use of the terms "party" and "faction." See David Hume, *The History of England from the Invasion of Julius Caesar to the Revolution in 1688* (Indianapolis: Liberty Fund, 1983), vol. 6, p. 123, and vol. 4, p, 290; and Mark G. Spencer, "Hume and Madison on Faction," *William and Mary Quarterly* 59, no. 4 (2002): 869–96.

12. Douglass Adair, "'That Politics May Be Reduced to a Science': David Hume, James Madison, and the Tenth Federalist," *Huntington Library Quarterly* 20, no. 4 (1957): 343–60.

13. James Madison, "Federalist no. 10," *New York Daily Advertiser*, 1787.

14. Marjorie Hershey, *Party Politics in America,* 17th edition (New York: Routledge, 2017), 19.

15. J. Austin Ranney, *Curing the Mischiefs of Faction: Party Reform in America* (Berkeley: University of California Press, 1975); see also Rosenblum, *On the Side of the Angels*, 189–90.

16. Ibid., xii, 18.

17. See Aldrich, *Why Parties*; Kathleen Bawn, "Constructing 'Us': Ideology, Coalition Politics, and False Consciousness," *American Journal of Political Science* 43, no. 2 (1999): 303–34.

18. Kathleen Bawn et al., "A Theory of Political Parties: Groups, Policy Demands and Nominations in American Politics," *Perspectives on Politics* 10, no. 3 (2012): 571–97.

19. Nelson W. Polsby, *Consequences of Party Reform* (New York: Oxford University Press, 1983); Bawn et al., "A Theory of Political Parties"; Cohen et al., *The Party Decides*; Marty Cohen et al., "Party versus Faction in the Reformed Presidential Nominating System," *PS: Political Science & Politics* 49, no. 4 (2016): 701–8.

20. Brown, *The Tea Party Divided*.

21. Matea Gold, "How National Tea Party Groups Missed the David Brat Boat," *Washington Post*, June 19, 2014, accessed March 15, 2019, at http://www

.washingtonpost.com/blogs/the-fix/wp/2014/06/10/how-national-tea-party-groups -missed-the-david-brat-boat/; James Warren, "Warren: House Majority Leader Eric Cantor's Defeat Shows Tea Party Is Not Dead," *New York Daily News*, June 11, 2014, accessed March 18, 2019, at https://www.nydailynews.com/news/ politics/warren-eric-cantor-defeat-shows-tea-party-not-dead-article-1.1824965 ?barcprox=true; Ezra Klein, "Eric Cantor Wasn't Beaten by the Tea Party," Vox, June 11, 2014, accessed March 14, 2019, at https://www.vox.com/2014/6/11/5799710/ Eric-Cantor-beaten-tea-party; Martina Stewart, "Tea Party Groups Target Senate after Presidential 'Disappointments,'" CNN, March 29, 2012, accessed March 1, 2019, at https://www.cnn.com/2012/ 03/29/politics/tea-party-election/index.html.

22. Michael Barber, "Donation Motivations: Testing Theories of Access and Ideology," *Political Research Quarterly* 69, no. 1 (2016): 148–59; Tim Groseclose and James M Snyder, "Buying Supermajorities," *American Political Science Review* 90, no. 2 (1996): 303–15; Richard L. Hall and Frank W. Wayman, "Buying Time: Moneyed Interests and the Mobilization of Bias in Congressional Committees," *American Political Science Review* 84, no. 3 (1990): 797–820.

23. As Schattschneider argued, interest groups (e.g. "pressure" groups) seek the adoption of pet policies, but without nominating candidates, fighting campaigns, or attempting to gain control of government; those aims are the domain of parties. See Schattschneider, *Party Government*, 187. See also Denise L. Baer and David A. Bositis, *Elite Cadres and Party Coalitions: Representing the Public in Party Politics* (Westport, CT: Greenwood Press, 1988); Jack L Walker, *Mobilizing Interest Groups in America: Patrons, Professions, and Social Movements* (Ann Arbor: University of Michigan Press, 1991).

24. Jo Freeman, "Resource Mobilization and Strategy: A Model for Analyzing Social Movement Organization Actions," in *The Dynamics of Social Movements*, ed. Mayer N. Zald and John D. McCarthy (Cambridge, MA: Winthrop Publishers, 1979), 167–89.

25. Rick Klein, "Democrats Seek to Own 'Occupy Wall Street' Movement," ABC News, October 10, 2011; accessed March 15, 2019, at https://abcnews.go .com/Politics/democrats-seek-occupy-wall-street-movement/story?id=14701337.

26. For an example of the benefits of considering different types of organization in tandem, see Daniel Schlozman, *When Movements Anchor Parties: Electoral Alignments in American History* (Princeton, NJ: Princeton University Press, 2015).

27. Michael T. Heaney and Fabio Rojas, *Party in the Street: The Antiwar Movement and the Democratic Party after 9/11* (Cambridge: Cambridge University Press, 2015).

28. Lee Ann Banaszak, *Why Movements Succeed or Fail: Opportunity, Culture, and the Struggle for Woman Suffrage* (Princeton, NJ: Princeton University Press, 1996); Alec Barbrook and Christine Bolt, *Power and Protest in American*

Life (New York: St. Martin's Press, 1980); William A. Gamson, *The Strategy of Social Protest* (Homewood, IL: Dorsey Press, 1975).

29. Alex Shepard, "It's Not Bernie Sanders's Job to Unify the Democratic Party," *New Republic*, May 20, 2016; accessed March 15, 2019, at https://newrepublic.com/article/133642/its-not-bernie-sanderss-job-unify-democratic-party; Reid Wilson, "The Three Republican Lanes: Establishment, Values, Change," *Morning Consult*, February 20, 2016; accessed March 14, 2019, at https://morningconsult.com/2016/02/20/ the-three-republican-lanes-establishment-values-change/.

30. Clyde Wilcox and Carin Robinson, *Onward Christian Soldiers? The Religious Right in American Politics* (New York: Routledge, 2011).

31. Baer and Bositis, *Elite Cadres and Party Coalitions*; Schlozman, *When Movements Anchor Parties*.

32. Duane Murray Oldfield, *The Right and the Righteous: The Christian Right Confronts the Republican Party* (New York: Rowman & Littlefield, 1996).

33. For an extended discussion of this overlap, see Michael Lienesch, *In the Beginning: Fundamentalism, the Scopes Trial, and the Making of the Antievolution Movement* (Chapel Hill: University of North Carolina Press, 2007).

34. Kari A. Frederickson, *The Dixiecrat Revolt and the End of the Solid South, 1932–1968* (Chapel Hill: University of North Carolina Press, 2001), 3.

35. Ruth Bloch Rubin, *Building the Bloc: Intraparty Organization in the US Congress* (Cambridge: Cambridge University Press, 2017).

36. Frederickson, *The Dixiecrat Revolt and the End of the Solid South*, 7–8.

37. Ibid., 154.

38. Geoffrey Kabaservice, *Rule and Ruin: The Downfall of Moderation and the Destruction of the Republican Party, from Eisenhower to the Tea Party* (New York: Oxford University Press, 2012), 25.

39. Nicole Hemmer, *Messengers of the Right: Conservative Media and the Transformation of American Politics* (Philadelphia: University of Pennsylvania Press, 2016); Kabaservice, *Rule and Ruin*.

40. DiSalvo, *Engines of Change*, 77–78.

41. John R. Petrocik, "Realignment: New Party Coalitions and the Nationalization of the South," *Journal of Politics* 49, no. 2 (1987): 347–75; Carmines and Stimson, *Issue Evolution*; Geoffrey C. Layman, Thomas Carsey, John Green, Richard Herrera, and Rosalyn Cooperman, "Activists and Conflict Extension in American Party Politics," *American Political Science Review* 104, no. 2 (2010): 324–46; Noel, *Political Ideologies and Political Parties in America*; David Hopkins and Matt Grossman, *Asymmetric Politics: Ideological Republicans and Group Interest Democrats* (New York: Oxford University Press, 2016); David Hopkins and Matt Grossman, "Ideological Republicans and Group Interest Democrats: The Asymmetry of American Party Politics," *Perspectives on Politics* 13, no. 1 (2015): 119–39; Levendusky, *The Partisan Sort*.

42. Or at least these were the official positions of the libertarian interest groups that provided support for the early Tea Party, such as FreedomWorks and Americans for Prosperity. See Burghart, "View from the Top"; Lo, "Astroturf versus Grass Roots"; Armey and Kibbe, *Give Us Liberty*; and Theda Skocpol and Alexander Hertel-Fernandez, "The Koch Network and Republican Party Extremism," *Perspectives on Politics* 14, no. 3 (2016): 681–99.

43. Williamson and Skocpol, *The Tea Party and the Remaking of Republican Conservatism*.

Chapter Three

1. Bailey, Mummolo, and Noel, "The Tea Party and Congressional Representation: Tracking the Influence of Activists, Groups and Elites"; Christopher F. Karpowitz, J. Quin Monson, Kelly D. Patterson, and Jeremy C. Pope, "Tea Time in America? The Impact of the Tea Party Movement on the 2010 Midterm Elections," *PS: Political Science & Politics* 44, no. 2 (2011): 303–9.

2. James E. Campbell, "Explaining Presidential Losses in Midterm Congressional Elections," *Journal of Politics* 47, no. 4 (1985): 1140–57; David W. Brady, John F. Cogan, Brian J. Gaines, and Douglas Rivers, "The Perils of Presidential Support: How the Republicans Took the House in the 1994 Midterm Elections," *Political Behavior* 18, no. 4 (1996): 345–67; Alan I. Abramowitz, "How Large a Wave? Using the Generic Ballot to Forecast the 2010 Midterm Elections," *PS: Political Science & Politics* 43, no. 4 (2010): 631–32.

3. Alan Abramowitz, "Grand Old Tea Party: Partisan Polarization and the Rise of the Tea Party Movement," in *Steep: The Precipitous Rise of the Tea Party*, ed. Lawrence Rosenthal and Christine Trost (Berkeley: University of California Press, 2012); Steven J. Rosenstone, Roy Behr, and Edward H. Lazarus, *Third Parties in America: Citizen Response to Major Party Failure* (Princeton, NJ: Princeton University Press, 1984); Jacobson, "The President, the Tea Party, and Voting Behavior in 2010"; Williamson and Skocpol, *The Tea Party and the Remaking of Republican Conservatism*.

4. Even studies designed to directly assess the views of Tea Partiers, such as Parker and Barreto's 2010 Multi-State Study of Race and Politics, could not circumvent the issue of sampling activists. For more information about this survey, see Parker and Barreto, *Change They Can't Believe In*.

5. Thomas M. Carsey, John C. Green, Richard Herrera, and Geoffrey C. Layman, "State Party Context and Norms among Delegates at the 2000 National Party Conventions," *State Politics and Policy Quarterly* 6, no. 3 (2006): 247–71; Layman et al. 2010.

6. I fielded the VPS between November 15 and December 15, 2013, following the 2013 Virginia Republican nominating convention. The survey was conducted

via Qualtrics and had one follow-up reminder, after which the Republican Party of Virginia requested that I cease and desist from further dissemination of the survey due to concerns that I was not a university researcher, but a mole planted by the Obama administration. Nevertheless, the survey received 1,600 responses (a 30 percent response rate).

7. I use respondents' full names only when the respondents were known public figures and I was granted permission to do so. Respondents who were not public figures, but who granted me permission to use their names, are referred to by their first name and last initial. Respondents who requested anonymity have been assigned pseudonyms; the first appearance of each pseudonym is denoted by an asterisk.

8. Although many 9/12 groups consider themselves to be part of the Tea Party, and though many Tea Partiers consider 9/12 to be part of their movement, Donnelly was careful to emphasize that the 9/12 movement is not specifically affiliated with the Tea Party.

9. This was a split-level experiment. Respondents received only one of these options.

Chapter Four

1. Richard Cohen, "Hanging in the Vapors," *Real Clear Politics*, October 26, 2010, accessed March 18, 2019, at https://www.realclearpolitics.com/articles/2010/10/26/anger_hanging_in_the_vapors_107728.html.

2. Paul Staniland, *Networks of Rebellion: Explaining Insurgent Cohesion and Collapse* (Ithaca, NY: Cornell University Press, 2014).

3. Mark Barabak, "The Earthquake That Toppled Eric Cantor: How Did It Happen?" *Los Angeles Times*, June 11, 2014, accessed March 14, 2019, at https://www.latimes.com/nation/politics/ politicsnow/la-pn-earthquake-toppled-cantor-20140611-story.html.

4. Rachel Blum, "Wait, the Tea Party's Back? Lessons from Eric Cantors Defeat," Mischiefs of Faction, June 2014, http://www.mischiefsoffaction.com/2014/06/wait-tea-partys-back-lessons-from-eric.html.

5. Many Tea Party sites organized these outgoing links in distinct sections, such as blog rolls or "further reading" sections. Less sophisticated sites displayed these links on their main pages.

6. SNA encompasses a set of methodological techniques geared toward studying the connections between actors, such as the relationships between interest groups, between lobbyists and members of Congress, among terrorist cells, and, for our purposes, between Tea Party groups and other political organizations. For examples, see Janet M. Box-Steffensmeier and Dino P. Christenson, "The Evolution and Formation of Amicus Curiae Networks," Social Networks 36

(2014): 82–96; Wendy K. Tam Cho and James H. Fowler, "Legislative Success in a Small World: Social Network Analysis and the Dynamics of Congressional Legislation," Journal of Politics 72, no. 1 (2010): 124–35; James H. Fowler, "Connecting the Congress: A Study of Cosponsorship Networks," Political Analysis 14, no. 4 (2006): 456–87; Gregory Koger, Seth Masket, and Hans Noel, "Partisan Webs: Information Exchange and Party Networks," British Journal of Political Science 39, no. 3 (2009): 633–53; Hans Noel, Seth E. Masket, and Gregory Koger, "Cooperative Party Factions in American Politics," American Politics Research 38, no. 1 (December 2009): 33–53; Jennifer Nicoll Victor and Gregory Koger, "Financing Friends: How Lobbyists Create a Web of Relationships among Members of Congress," Interest Groups & Advocacy 5, no. 3 (May 2016): 224–62; Valdis E. Krebs, "Mapping Networks of Terrorist Cells," Connections 24, no. 3 (2002): 43–52; Mario Diani and Doug McAdam, Social Movements and Networks: Relational Approaches to Collective Action (New York: Oxford University Press, 2003); Heaney and Rojas, Party in the Street.

7. I used the "walktrap" community detection algorithm, as implemented in the igraph package in the statistical program R. Two communities were isolates, and dropped from the analysis, resulting in 270 communities.

8. Specifically, I calculated in-degree centrality using the implementation in the igraph package in R.

9. For more on traditional party organization, see Paul Allen Beck, "Environment and Party: The Impact of Political and Demographic County Characteristics on Party Behavior," American Political Science Review 68, no. 3 (September 1974): 1229–44; Melody Ara Crowder-Meyer, "Local Parties, Local Candidates, and Women's Representation: How County Parties Affect Who Runs for and Wins Political Office" (PhD diss., Princeton University, 2010); John C. Green and Daniel J. Coffey, The State of the Parties: The Changing Role of Contemporary American Parties, 6th. ed. (New York: Rowman & Littlefield, 2011); Mayhew, Placing Parties in American Politics.

10. For cases in which not all of a community's members were easily categorized, I classified each community based on characteristics of its twenty most central members.

Chapter Five

1. David E. Campbell and Robert D. Putnam, "Crashing the Tea Party," New York Times, August 16, 2011, accessed March 1, 2019, at https://www.nytimes .com/2011/08/17/opinion/ crashing-the-tea-party.html; The Tea Party and Religion, technical report, Pew Research Center, February 23, 2011, http://www .pewforum.org/2011/02/23/ tea-party-and-religion/; David Sessions, "Tea Party: Is It the Christian Right in Disguise?" Daily Beast, August 8, 2011, accessed

March 15, 2019, at https://www.thedailybeast.com/tea-party-is-it-the-christian-right-in-disguise.

2. Emily Ekins and David Kirby, "Libertarian Roots of the Tea Party," *Cato Institute Policy Analysis* 705 (2012).

3. Abramowitz, "Grand Old Tea Party"; Williamson and Skocpol, *The Tea Party and the Remaking of Republican Conservatism.*

4. Leslie Kaufman and Kate Zernike, "Activists Fight Green Projects, Seeing U.N. Plot," *New York Times*, February 3, 2012, accessed March 14, 2019, at https://www.nytimes.com/2012/02/04/us/activists-fight-green-projects-seeing-un-plot.html?mtrref=www.google.com&gwh=CFED7F74E2F8D0AB3862E103381DBDA5&gwt=pay.

5. Parker and Barreto, *Change They Can't Believe In*; Seymour Martin Lipset and Earl Raab, *The Politics of Unreason: Right-Wing Extremism in America, 1790–1970* (New York: Harper & Row, 1978); Lawrence Bobo and Vincent L Hutchings, "Perceptions of Racial Group Competition: Extending Blumer's Theory of Group Position to a Multiracial Social Context," *American Sociological Review*, 1996, 951–72; Robert A. LeVine and Donald T. Campbell, *Ethnocentrism: Theories of Conflict, Ethnic Attitudes, and Group Behavior* (New York: John Wiley & Sons, 1972); Joseph R. Gusfield, *Symbolic Crusade: Status Politics and the American Temperance Movement* (Champaign: University of Illinois Press, 1963); John T. Jost et al., "Political Conservatism as Motivated Social Cognition," *Psychological Bulletin* 129, no. 3 (2003): 339.

6. Maureen A. Craig and Jennifer Richeson, "On the Precipice of a 'Majority-Minority' America: Perceived Status Threat from the Racial Demographic Shift Affects White Americans' Political Ideology," *Psychological Science* 25, no. 6 (2014): 1189–97; Brenda Major, Alison Blodorn, and Gregory Major Blascovich, "The Threat of Increasing Diversity: Why Many White Americans Support Trump in the 2016 Presidential Election," *Group Processes and Intergroup Relations*, 2016, 1–10; Matthew C. MacWilliams, "Who Decides When the Party Doesn't: Authoritarian Voters and the Rise of Trump," *PS: Political Science and Politics* 29, no. 4 (2016): 716–21; Michael Tesler, John Sides, and Lynn Vavrek, *Identity Crisis: The 2016 Presidential Campaign and the Battle for the Meaning of America* (Princeton, NJ: Princeton University Press, 2018); Rachel Marie Blum and Christopher Sebastian Parker, "Trump-ing Foreign Affairs: Status Threat and Foreign Policy Preferences on the Right," *Perspectives on Politics* 17, no. 3 (2019): 737–55.

7. McCarty, Poole, and Rosenthal, "Income Redistribution and the Realignment of American Politics"; Rohde, *Parties and Leaders in the Postreform House*; Aldrich, *Why Parties?*; Adams, "Abortion: Evidence of an Issue Evolution"; Layman, *The Great Divide*; Abramowitz and Saunders, "Ideological Realignment in the US Electorate."

8. Noel, *Political Ideologies and Political Parties in America*, 41.

9. Ibid.

10. John Clifford Green, James L. Guth, and Corwin E. Smidt, *Religion and the Culture Wars: Dispatches from the Front* (Lanham, MD: Rowman & Littlefield, 1996); John C. Green, Mark J. Rozell, and Clyde Wilcox, "Social Movements and Party Politics: The Case of the Christian Right," *Journal for the Scientific Study of Religion* 40, no. 3 (2001): 413–26; Elizabeth A. Cook, Ted G. Jelen, and Clyde Wilcox, *Between Two Absolutes: Public Opinion and the Politics of Abortion* (Boulder, CO: Westview Press, 1992); Andrew Hartman, *A War for the Soul of America: A History of the Culture Wars* (Chicago: University of Chicago Press, 2015).

11. John Dombrink, *The Twilight of Social Conservatism: American Culture Wars in the Obama Era* (New York: NYU Press, 2015).

12. Emily Ekins and David Kirby, "Libertarian Roots of the Tea Party," *Cato Institute Policy Analysis,* no. 705 (2012).

13. Parker and Barreto, *Change They Can't Believe In*; Lisa Disch, "The Tea Party: A "White Citizenship" Movement?" in *Steep: The Precipitous Rise of the Tea Party*, ed. Lawrence Rosenthal and Christine Trost (Berkeley: University of California Press, 2012), 133–51.

14. Nicole Hemmer, *Messengers of the Right: Conservative Media and the Transformation of American Politics* (Philadelphia: University of Pennsylvania Press, 2016); Lilliana Mason, *Uncivil Agreement: How Politics Became Our Identity* (Chicago: University of Chicago Press, 2018); Parker and Barreto, *Change They Can't Believe In;* Joseph Gusfield, *Symbolic Crusade: Status Politics and the American Temperance Movement.*

15. See Zernike, *Boiling Mad.*

16. Dick Armey and Matt Kibbe, *Give Us Liberty: A Tea Party Manifesto* (New York: William Morrow, 2010), 27.

17. Molly Ball, October 9, 2013, "The Koch's Can't Control the Monster They Created," *Atlantic*, https://www.theatlantic.com/politics/archive/2013/10/the-kochs -cant-control-the-monster-they-created/280435/.

18. Interview with Bill Redpath conducted on August 28, 2013.

19. After experimenting with different numbers of topics and comparing output, I found that 100 was the number at which topics were still meaningfully distinct, but not underfitted.

20. Jay Heflin, "Tea Party Primary Wins Give Boost to 'Fair Tax' Plan to Kill Federal Income Taxes," *The Hill*, September 20, 2010, https://thehill.com/policy/ finance/119655-tea-party-primary-wins-give-boost-to-fair-tax-reform-proposal.

21. Julia Azari, "From Wallace to Trump: The Evolution of Law and Order," FiveThirtyEight, March 15, 2016, https://fivethirtyeight.com/features/from -wallace-to-trump-the-evolution-of-law-and-order/.

22. Parker and Barreto, *Change They Can't Believe In*, introduction.

23. Blum and Parker, "Trump-Ing Foreign Affairs: Status Threat and Foreign Policy Preferences on the Right."

Chapter Six

1. Gervais and Morris, 2018; Rubin, *Building the Bloc*; Zack Beauchamp, "The Republican Party versus Democracy," Vox, December 17, 2018, https: // www.vox.com/policy-and-politics/2018/12/17/18092210/republican-gop-trump -2020-democracy-threat.

2. On September 25, 2015, John Boehner abruptly resigned from his position as speaker of the House, ending his twenty-four-year tenure in Congress. As he explained: "I've got plenty of people following me but this turmoil that's been churning now for a couple of months, it's not good for the members and it's not good for the institution." See Dana Bash et al., "House Speaker John Boehner: I Decided Today Is the Day," CNN, September 15, 2015, accessed March 15, 2019, at https: //www.cnn.com/2015/09/25/politics/john-boehner-resigning-as-speaker/ index.html.

3. Gayle King, "Paul Ryan's Interview with 'CBS This Morning' (full transcript)," CBS, April 12, 2018, accessed March 15, 2019, at https://www.cbsnews .com/news/paul-ryan-trump-stepping-down-cbs-interview-full-transcript-today -2018–04–12/.

4. Nolan McCarty, Keith T. Poole, and Howard Rosenthal, *Polarized America: The Dance of Ideology and Unequal Riches* (Cambridge, MA: MIT Press, 2008); Sinclair, *Party Wars*; Data Labs Team, *Partisan Conflict and Congressional Outreach*, technical report (Pew Research Center, February 23, 2017), http://www.people-press.org/wp-content/uploads/sites/4/2017/02/LabsReport_ FINALreport.pdf.

5. As of 2016, the House boasted four hundred caucuses that had registered with the House Committee on Administration (and many more that did not register)—meaning that there were likely more caucuses than members of the House. See Nils Ringe, Jennifer Nicoll Victor, and Christopher J Carman, *Bridging the Information Gap: Legislative Member Organizations as Social Networks in the United States and the European Union* (Ann Arbor: University of Michigan Press, 2013); Jennifer Nicoll Victor, "Can Congress Build Bipartisanship through Caucuses?" The Conversation, September 14, 2016, accessed March 15, 2019, at https://theconversation.com/can-congress-build-bipartisanship-through -caucuses-64286.

6. Rubin, *Building the Bloc*.

7. John Aldrich and David W. Rohde, "The Logic of Conditional Party Government," in *Congress Reconsidered*, 7th, ed. Lawrence C. Dodd and Bruce

Oppenheimer (Washington: Congressional Quarterly Press, 2000), 269–92; William T. Bianco and Itai Sened, "Uncovering Evidence of Conditional Party Government: Reassessing Majority Party Influence in Congress and State Legislatures," *American Political Science Review* 99, no. 3 (2005): 361–71.

8. Rubin, *Building the Bloc*, 23.

9. A few earlier congressional factions, namely LaFollette's insurgents in 1923 and the Democratic Study Group of the 1950s and '60s, also challenged their host parties in order to gain concessions. See DiSalvo, *Engines of Change*; Eric Schickler, *Disjointed Pluralism: Institutional Innovation and the Development of the U.S. Congress* (Princeton, NJ: Princeton University Press, 2001).

10. Jake Sherman, "Bachmann Forms Tea Party Caucus," Politico, July 16, 2010, accessed March 16, 2019, https://www.politico.com/story/2010/07/bachmann-forms-tea-party-caucus-039848.

11. Daniel Newhauser, "What Happened to the Tea Party Caucus?" *Roll Call*, May 20, 2013, accessed March 15, 2019, at https://www.rollcall.com/news/what_happened_to_the_tea_party_caucus-223309-1.html.

12. Susan Ferrechio, "Libertarian Wing of GOP Gains Strength in Congress," *Washington Examiner*, January 24, 2014, accessed March 16, 2019, at https://www.washingtonexaminer.com/ libertarian-wing-of-gop-gains-strength-in-congress.

13. Joel Gehrke, "Meet the Freedom Caucus," *National Review*, January 26, 2015, accessed March 15, 2019, at https://www.nationalreview.com/2015/01/meet-freedom-caucus-joel-gehrke/.

14. A breakdown of membership by Congress can be found in the technical appendix. Unlike the Tea Party and the Liberty Caucus, the HFC did not and does not publish an official list of its members. To get around this, I created a membership list from the public statements of those representatives who are explicitly affiliated with the caucus, which I then cross-checked with the list created by the Pew Research Center. Drew Desilver, "What Is the House Freedom Caucus, and Who's in It?" Pew Research Center, October 20, 2015, accessed March 14, 2019, at http://www.pewresearch.org/fact-tank/2015/10/20/house-freedom-caucus-what-is-it-and-whos-in-it/. Sean Theriault defines the Tea Party in Congress to include not only those who were part of the original Tea Party caucus, but also those who were part of the Liberty Caucus or the HFC. See Sean M. Theriault, *The Gingrich Senators: The Roots of Partisan Warfare in Congress* (New York: Oxford University Press, 2013).

15. Early work on the Tea Party and Congress focused on whether the Tea Party contributed to Republican victories in the 2010 midterm elections, and on how it influenced the ensuing 112th Congress. See Bailey, Mummolo, and Noel, "The Tea Party and Congressional Representation"; Jon R. Bond, Richard Fleisher, and Nathan A. Ilderton, "Did the Tea Party Win the House for the Republicans in the 2010 House Elections?" *Forum* 10, no. 2 (July 2012): 1540–8884.

This scholarship defined Tea Partiers as members who were endorsed by national Tea Party groups or were members of the Tea Party caucus. Gervais and Morris extended this definition to include self-identifiers and recipients of endorsements and donations, along with multiple classifications of Tea Party types. I do not rely on self-identification or Tea Party PAC–centric metrics, due to the tendency of those approaches to overamplify the surge of energy surrounding the Tea Party in its earlier protest-oriented phase. The activity of Tea Party interest groups faded after 2010 as these groups' prominence faded; and the Tea Party label grew increasingly obsolete in the 113th and 114th Congresses, commensurate with the faction's success in infiltrating its host party. For example, some members, such as John Boehner, semiofficially associated themselves with the Tea Party early on, only to distance themselves from it later. See David Herszenhorn, "Congress Now Has a 'Tea Party Caucus,'" Caucus Blog of the *New York Times*, July 20, 2010, accessed March 16, 2019, at https://thecaucus.blogs.nytimes .com/2010/07/20/congress-now-has-a-tea-party-caucus/?mtrref=www.google .com&gwh=CEDAB5630C222434BF279F49C683B7AA&gwt=pay).

16. The classification of these votes follows that of Stephen A. Jessee and Sean M. Theriault, "The Two Faces of Congressional Roll-Call Voting," *Party Politics* 20, no. 6 (October 2012): 836–48. Jessee and Theriault used the VOTE variable from the PIPC Roll Call Database; David Rohde and Michael H. Crespin, Retrieved August 2017, *Political Institutions and Public Choice Roll-Call Database*, retrieved from https://ou.edu/carlalbertcenter/research/pipc-votes/. Votes categorized as 24, 52–64, and 66–99 were coded as procedural; 21–23 and 25–29 as amendments, and 1–19, 30–34, and 65 as substantive/final passage.

17. Again, I used walktrap, a hierarchical clustering algorithm that maximizes modularity.

18. Margaret E. Roberts, Brandon Stewart, and Dustin Tingley, "stm: R Package for Structural Topic Models," *Journal of Statistical Software* 10, no. 2 (2014): 1–40.

19. For ideology, I used the first-dimension scores for DW-Nominate. See Jeffrey B. Lewis et al., "Voteview: Congressional Roll-Call Votes Database," Voteview.com, retrieved 2018. For district competitiveness, I used 2012 partisan voting index scores. See David Wasserman, "Introducing the 2012 Cook Political Report Partisan Voter Index," *Cook Political Report*, October 11, 2012. For the year variable, I included the year the press release was issued.

20. Keith T. Poole and Howard Rosenthal, "The Polarization of American Politics," *Journal of Politics* 46, no. 4 (November 1984): 1061.

21. Keith T. Poole and Howard Rosenthal, *Congress: A Political-Economic History of Roll Call Voting* (New York: Oxford University Press, 1997); James M. Snyder and Tim Groseclose, "Estimating Party Influence in Congressional Roll-Call Voting," *American Journal of Political Science* 44, no. 2 (2000): 193–

211; Gary W. Cox and Keith T. Poole, "On Measuring Partisanship in Roll-Call Voting: The U.S. House of Representatives, 1877–1999," *American Journal of Political Science* 46, no. 3 (July 2002): 477–89.

22. James M. Snyder, Stephen Ansolabehere, and C. Stewart, "The Effects of Party and Preferences on Congressional Roll Call Voting," *Legislative Studies Quarterly* 26, no. 4 (2001): 533–72.

23. Gervais and Morris, *Reactionary Republicanism*.

24. Snyder, Ansolabehere, and Stewart, "The Effects of Party and Preferences on Congressional Roll Call Voting"; Gary W. Cox and Matthew D. McCubbins, *Legislative Leviathan: Party Government in the House* (Berkeley, CA: University of California Press, 1993); Cox and Poole, "On Measuring Partisanship in Roll-Call Voting"; Jeffery A. Jenkins, Michael H. Crespin, and Jamie L. Carson, "Parties as Procedural Coalitions in Congress: An Examination of Differing Career Tracks," *Legislative Studies Quarterly* 30 (2005): 365–90; Rohde, *Parties and Leaders in the Postreform House*; Snyder and Groseclose, "Estimating Party Influence in Congressional Roll-Call Voting"; Theriault, *Party Polarization in Congress*.

25. Jessee and Theriault, "The Two Faces of Congressional Roll-Call Voting."

26. Mayhew, *The Electoral Connection*; Gregory Koger, "Position Taking and Cosponsorship in the U.S. House," *Legislative Studies Quarterly* 28, no. 2 (May 2003): 225–46; Daniel Kessler and Keith Krehbiel, "Dynamics of Cosponsorship," *American Political Science Review* 90, no. 3 (1996): 555–66; Glen S. Krutz, "Issues and Institutions: 'Winnowing' in the U.S. Congress," *American Journal of Political Science* 49, no. 2 (April 2005): 313–26; Rick K. Wilson and Cheryl D. Young, "Cosponsorship in the U.S. Congress," *Legislative Studies Quarterly* 22, no. 1 (February 1997): 25–43; Jonathan Woon, "Bill Sponsorship in Congress: The Moderating Effect of Agenda Positions on Legislative Proposals," *Journal of Politics* 70, no. 1 (2008): 201–16.

27. James H. Fowler, "Legislative Cosponsorship Networks in the US House and Senate," *Social Networks* 28 (2006): 454–65; James E. Campbell, "Cosponsoring Legislation in the U.S. Congress," *Legislative Studies Quarterly* 7, no. 3 (August 1982): 415–22.

28. Gervais and Morris, *Reactionary Republicanism*.

29. Mayhew, *The Electoral Connection*; Justin Grimmer, Sean J. Westwood, and Solomon Messing, *The Impression of Influence: Legislator Communication, Representation, and Democratic Accountability* (Princeton, NJ: Princeton University Press, 2014).

30. At conventional levels of statistical significance.

31. A few topics were entirely made up of leftover .html markup and other filler. These were omitted from this analysis.

32. The magnitude of the coefficients is relatively small, ranging from -0.04 to

+0.04, as it was for all coefficients used in these models due to the sheer size of the data.

33. Rubin, *Building the Bloc*, 303.

Chapter Seven

1. Michael Reynolds, "Photo Essay: Signs of the Tea-Party Protests," *Time*, accessed March 18, 2019, at http://content.time.com/time/photogallery/0,29307 ,1922169,00.html; Chris Good, "Signs of the Times: Slogans and Images from the Tea Party Rally," *Atlantic*, September 13, 2010, https://www.theatlantic.com/ politics/archive/2010/09/signs-of-the-times-slogans-and-images-from-the-tea -party-rally/62885/; Timothy Noah, "The Medicare-Isn't-Government Meme," *Slate*, August 5, 2009, https://slate.com/news-and-politics/2009/ 08/help-slate-track-the-medicare-isn-t-government-meme.html.

2. E.g., Vanessa Williamson, "What the Tea Party Tells Us about the Trump Presidency," *Brookings Institution's FixGov*, November 2016,

3. Williamson and Skocpol, *The Tea Party and the Remaking of Republican Conservatism*; Parker and Barreto, *Change They Can't Believe In*; Gervais and Morris, *Reactionary Republicanism*.

4. Parker and Barreto, *Change They Can't Believe In*; Gervais and Morris, *Reactionary Republicanism*.

5. Parker and Barreto, *Change They Can't Believe In*; Gusfield, *Symbolic Crusade*; Richard Hofstadter, *The Paranoid Style in American Politics and Other Essays* (Cambridge, MA: Harvard University Press, 1965).

6. Parker and Barreto, *Change They Can't Believe In*.

7. E.g., Anup Kumar, "The Tea Party Movement: The Problem of Populism as a Discursive Political Practice," *Javnost-The Public* 18, no. 4 (2011): 55–71; Chip Berlet, "Taking Tea Parties Seriously: Corporate Globalization, Populism, and Resentment," *Perspectives on Global Development and Technology* 10, no. 1 (2011): 11–29; Anton Pelinka, "Right-Wing Populism: Concept and Typology," in *Right-Wing Populism in Europe: Politics and Discourse*, ed. Ruth Wobak, Majid Khosravinik, and Brigitte Mral (London: Bloomsbury, 2013): 3–22.

8. Cas Mudde, "The Populist Zeitgeist," *Government and Opposition* 39 (2004); John Judis and Ruy Teixeira, *The Emerging Democratic Majority* (New York: Simon & Schuster, 2002).

9. William A. Galston, "The Liberal Faction of the Democratic Party Is Growing, New Polling Shows," *Brookings*, January 9, 2019, accessed March 18, 2019, at https://www.brookings.edu/blog/fixgov/2019/01/11/the-liberal-faction-of-the -democratic-party-is-growingnew-polling -shows/; David A. Graham, "How Far Have the Democrats Moved to the Left?" *Atlantic*, November 5, 2018, accessed

March 18, 2019, at https://www.theatlantic.com/politics/archive/2018/11/democratic -voters-move-leftward-range-issues/574834/; Adam Gabbatt, "'Tea Party of the Left': Bernie Sanders' Ethos Endures in Impending Trump Era," *Guardian*, November 15, 2016, accessed March 18, 2019, at https://www.theguardian.com/us -news/2016/nov/15/bernie-sanders-progressive-activism-trump-protests.

10. Bob Fredericks, "Ocasio-Cortez Pushes for a Leftist Revolt in the Democratic Party," *New York Post*, November 19, 2018, accessed March 18, 2019, at https: //nypost.com/2018/11/19/ocasio-cortez-pushes-for-a-leftist-revolt-in-the -democratic-party/.

11. Eric Garcia, "Lipinski Warns about Tea Party of the Left," *Roll Call*, March 5, 2018, accessed March 18, 2019, at https://www.rollcall.com/news/ politics/lipinski-warns-about-tea-party-of-the-left.

12. Tara Golshan and Ella Nilsen, "Progressives in Congress Could Be the Tea Party of the Left," Vox, December 4, 2018, accessed March 18, 2019, at https:// www.vox.com/policy-and-politics/2018/12/4/18103476/progressives-congress -ocasio-cortez-freedom-caucus.

13. Seth Ackerman, "A Blueprint for a New Party," *Jacobin*, November 2016, accessed March 18, 2019, at https://www.jacobinmag.com/2016/11/bernie -sanders-democratic-labor-party-ackerman.

14. Hopkins and Grossman, *Asymmetric Politics*.

Technical Appendixes

1. Ballotpedia, "Ballot Access Requirements for Political Parties in Ohio."

2. Larry J. Sabato, Kyle Kondik, and Geoffrey Skelley, "So What Just Happened in Virginia? A Brief History of Old Dominion Nomination Battles," *University of Virginia Center for Politics*, May 2013, accessed May 1, 2018, at http:// www.centerforpolitics.org/crystalball/articles/are-primaries-or-conventions -more-successful-for-a-party/.

3. Pascal Pons and Matthieu Latapy, "Computing Communities in Large Networks Using Random Walks," *Journal of Graph Algorithms Applications* 10, no. 2 (2006): 191–218.

4. Daniel J Hopkins and Gary King, "A Method of Automated Nonparametric Content Analysis for Social Science," *American Journal of Political Science* 54, no. 1 (2009): 229–47; Daniel J. Hopkins, "The Exaggerated Life of Death Panels? The Limited but Real Influence of Elite Rhetoric in the 2009–2010 Health Care Debate," *Political Behavior* 40, no. 3 (2018): 681–709; Justin Grimmer and Brandon M. Stewart, "Text as Data: The Promise and Pitfalls of Automatic Content Analysis Methods for Political Texts," *Political Analysis* 21, no. 3 (2013): 267–97.

5. David M. Blei and John D. Lafferty, "Dynamic Topic Models," *Proceed-*

ings of the 23rd International Conference on Machine Learning, June 2006, 113–20.

6. Hopkins, "The Exaggerated Life of Death Panels?"; Jonathan Chang et al., "Reading Tea Leaves: How Humans Interpret Topic Models," *Neural Information Processing Systems* 22 (2009); Justin Grimmer and Gary King, "General Purpose Computer-Assisted Clustering and Conceptualization," *PNAS* 108, no. 7 (February 2011): 2643–50.

Bibliography

Abramowitz, Alan. *The Disappearing Center: Engaged Citizens, Polarization, and American Democracy.* New Haven: Yale University Press, 2010.

———. "Grand Old Tea Party: Partisan Polarization and the Rise of the Tea Party Movement." In *Steep: The Precipitous Rise of the Tea Party,* edited by Lawrence Rosenthal and Christine Trost. Berkeley: University of California Press, 2012.

———. "How Large a Wave? Using the Generic Ballot to Forecast the 2010 Midterm Elections." *PS: Political Science & Politics* 43, no. 4 (2010): 631–32.

Abramowitz, Alan I., and Kyle L. Saunders. "Ideological Realignment in the US Electorate." *Journal of Politics* 60, no. 3 (1998): 634–52.

Ackerman, Seth. "A Blueprint for a New Party." *Jacobin,* November 2016. Accessed March 18, 2019, at https://www.jacobinmag.com/2016/11/bernie-sanders-democratic-labor-party-ackerman.

Adair, Douglass. *Fame and the Founding Fathers: Essays by Douglass Adair.* Edited by Trevor Coulbourn. Indianapolis: Liberty Fund, 1998.

Adams, Greg D. "Abortion: Evidence of an Issue Evolution." *American Journal of Political Science,* 1997, 718–37.

Aldrich, John H. *Why Parties? The Origin and Transformation of Political Parties in America.* Chicago: University of Chicago Press, 1995.

Aldrich, John, and David W. Rohde. "The Logic of Conditional Party Government." In *Congress Reconsidered,* 7th edition, edited by Lawrence C. Dodd and Bruce Oppenheimer, 269–92. Washington: Congressional Quarterly Press, 2000.

Armey, Dick, and Matt Kibbe. *Give Us Liberty: A Tea Party Manifesto.* New York: William Morrow, 2011.

Azari, Julia. "From Wallace to Trump: The Evolution of Law and Order." FiveThirtyEight, March 15, 2016. Accessed September 1, 2019 at https://fivethirtyeight.com/features/from-wallace-to-trump-the-evolution-of-law-and-order/.

Baer, Denise L., and David A. Bositis. *Elite Cadres and Party Coalitions: Representing the Public in Party Politics.* New York: Greenwood, 1988.

Bailey, Michael, Jonathan Mummolo, and Hans Noel. "The Tea Party and Congressional Representation: Tracking the Influence of Activists, Groups and Elites." *American Politics Research* 20, no. 10 (2012): 1–3.

Ball, Molly. "The Kochs Can't Control the Monster They Created." *Atlantic*, October 9, 2013. Accessed September 1, 2019 at https://www.theatlantic.com/politics/archive/2013/10/the-kochs-cant-control-the-monster-they-created/280435/.

Ballotpedia. "Ballot Access Requirements for Political Parties in Ohio." Accessed March 15, 2019, at https://ballotpedia.org/Ballot_access_requirements_for_political_parties_in_Ohio.

Banaszak, Lee Ann. *Why Movements Succeed or Fail: Opportunity, Culture, and the Struggle for Woman Suffrage.* Princeton, NJ: Princeton University Press, 1996.

Barabak, Mark. "The Earthquake That Toppled Eric Cantor: How Did It Happen?" *Los Angeles Times*, June 11, 2014. Accessed March 14, 2019, at https://www.latimes.com/nation/politics/politicsnow/la-pn-earthquake-toppled-cantor-20140611-story.html.

Barber, Michael. "Donation Motivations: Testing Theories of Access and Ideology." *Political Research Quarterly* 69, no. 1 (2016): 148–59.

Barbrook, Alec, and Christine Bolt. *Power and Protest in American Life.* New York: St. Martin's Press, 1980.

Bartel, Bill. "Jackson Is Disappointed Rigell Won't Endorse Him." *Virginian-Pilot*, June 6, 2013. https://pilotonline.com/news/government/politics/article_9219c57d0d3d-572f-b3b0-cd791c0783f5.%20html.

Bash, Dana, Manu Raju, Deirdre Walsh, and Jeremy Diamond. "House Speaker John Boehner: I Decided Today Is the Day." CNN, September 15, 2015. Accessed March 15, 2019, at https://www.cnn.com/2015/09/25/politics/john-boehner-resigning-as-speaker/index.html.

Bawn, Kathleen. "Constructing 'Us': Ideology, Coalition Politics, and False Consciousness." *American Journal of Political Science* 43, no. 2 (1999): 303–34.

Bawn, Kathleen, Marty Cohen, David Karol, Seth Masket, Hans Noel, and John Zaller. "A Theory of Political Parties: Groups, Policy Demands and Nominations in American Politics." *Perspectives on Politics* 10, no. 3 (2012): 571–97.

Beauchamp, Zack. "The Republican Party versus Democracy." Vox, December 17, 2018. ht tps://www.vox.com/policy-and-politics/2018/12/17/18092210/republicangop-trump-2020-democracy-threat.

Beck, Paul Allen. "Environment and Party: The Impact of Political and Demographic County Characteristics on Party Behavior." *American Political Science Review* 68, no. 3 (September 1974): 1229–44.

Berlet, Chip. "Taking Tea Parties Seriously: Corporate Globalization, Populism, and Resentment." *Perspectives on Global Development and Technology* 10, no. 1 (2011): 11–29.

Bianco, William T., and Itai Sened. "Uncovering Evidence of Conditional Party Government: Reassessing Majority Party Influence in Congress and State Legislatures." *American Political Science Review* 99, no. 3 (2005): 361–71.

Bilaik, Carl. "How the Republican Field Dwindled From 17 to Donald Trump." FiveThirtyEight, May 5, 2016. Accessed August 9, 2019 at https://fivethirtyeight.com/features/how-the-republican-field-dwindled-from-17-to-donald-trump/.

Blake, Aaron. "Whip Count: Here's Where Republicans Stand on Trump's Controversial Travel Ban." *Washington Post*, January 29, 2017. Accessed April 10, 2018, at https://www.washingtonpost.com/news/the-fix/wp/2017/01/29/heres-where-republicans-stand-on-president-t%20?utm_term=.a4bf0681f98e.

Blei, David M., and John D. Lafferty. "Dynamic Topic Models." *Proceedings of the 23rd International Conference on Machine Learning*, June 2006, 113–20.

Blum, Rachel. "Wait, the Tea Party's Back? Lessons from Eric Cantor's Defeat." Mischiefs of Faction (Vox), June 2014. http://www.mischiefsoffaction.com/2014/06/wait-tea-partys-back-lessons-from-eric.html.

Blum, Rachel Marie, and Christopher Sebastian Parker. "Trump-ing Foreign Affairs: Status Threat and Foreign Policy Preferences on the Right." *Perspectives on Politics* 17, no. 3 (2019): 737-55.

Bobo, Lawrence, and Vincent L. Hutchings. "Perceptions of Racial Group Competition: Extending Blumer's Theory of Group Position to a Multiracial Social Context." *American Sociological Review*, 1996, 951–72.

Bolingbroke, Henry St. John Viscount. "The Idea of a Patriot King." In *The Works of Lord Bolingbroke: With a Life, Prepared Expressly for This Edition, Containing Additional Information Relative to His Personal and Public Character*. Philadelphia: Carey/Hart, 1841.

Bond, Jon R., Richard Fleisher, and Nathan A. Ilderton. "Did the Tea Party Win the House for the Republicans in the 2010 House Elections?" *The Forum* 10, no. 2 (July 2012): 1540–8884.

Box-Steffensmeier, Janet M., and Dino P. Christenson. "The Evolution and Formation of Amicus Curiae Networks." *Social Networks* 36 (2014): 82–96.

Brady, David W., John F. Cogan, Brian J. Gaines, and Douglas Rivers. "The Perils of Presidential Support: How the Republicans Took the House in the 1994 Midterm Elections." *Political Behavior* 18, no. 4 (1996): 345–67.

Brown, Heath. *The Tea Party Divided: The Hidden Diversity of a Maturing Movement*. ABC-CLIO, 2015.

Bump, Philip. "The 2016 GOP Presidential Race, Broken Down Into 5 'Lanes.'" *Washington Post*, March 25, 2015. Accessed August 9, 2019, at https://www.washingtonpost.com/news/the-fix/wp/2015/03/25/breaking-down-the-lanes-theory-of-the-2016-republican-field/?utm_term=.8a6665fcc54f.

Burghart, Devin. "View from the Top: Reports on Six National Tea Party Organizations." In *Steep: The Precipitous Rise of the Tea Party*, edited by Lawrence Rosenthal and Christine Trost. Berkeley: University of California Press, 2012.

Campbell, David E., and Robert D. Putnam. "Crashing the Tea Party." *New York Times*, August 16, 2011. Accessed March 1, 2019, at https://www.nytimes .com/2011/08/17/opinion/crashing-the-tea-party.html.

Campbell, James E. "Cosponsoring Legislation in the U.S. Congress." *Legislative Studies Quarterly* 7, no. 3 (August 1982): 415–22.

———. "Explaining Presidential Losses in Midterm Congressional Elections." *Journal of Politics* 47, no. 4 (1985): 1140–57.

Canon, David T. "The Year of the Outsider: Political Amateurs in the U.S. Congress." *The Forum* 8, no. 4 (January 2011).

Carmines, Edward G., and James A. Stimson. *Issue Evolution*. Princeton, NJ: Princeton University Press, 1989.

Carsey, Thomas M., John C. Green, Richard Herrera, Geoffrey C. Layman. "State Party Context and Norms among Delegates at the 2000 National Party Conventions." *State Politics and Policy Quarterly* 6, no. 3 (2006): 247–71.

Chang, Jonathan, Sean Gerrish, Chong Wang, Jordan L. Body-Graber, and David M. Blei. "Reading Tea Leaves: How Humans Interpret Topic Models." *Neural Information Processing Systems* 22 (2009).

Cohen, Marty, David Karol, Hans Noel, and John Zaller. *The Party Decides: Presidential Nominations before and after Reform*. Chicago: University of Chicago Press, 2008.

———. "Party versus Faction in the Reformed Presidential Nominating System." *PS: Political Science & Politics* 49, no. 4 (2016): 701–8.

Cohen, Richard. "Hanging in the Vapors." Real Clear Politics, October 26, 2010. Accessed March 18, 2019, at https://www.realclearpolitics.com/articles/2010/ 10/26/anger_hanging_in_the_vapors_107728.html.

Cook, Elizabeth A., Ted G. Jelen, and Clyde Wilcox. *Between Two Absolutes: Public Opinion and the Politics of Abortion*. Boulder, CO: Westview Press, 1992.

Cormack, Lindsey. "DCinbox: Capturing Every Congressional Constituent E-Newsletter from 2009 Onwards." *Legislative Scholar* 2, no. 1 (2017): 27–34.

Courser, Zachary. "The Tea Party at the Election." *The Forum* 8, no. 4 (June 2011).

Cox, Gary W., and Matthew D. McCubbins. *Legislative Leviathan: Party Government in the House*. Berkeley: University of California Press, 1993.

Cox, Gary W., and Keith T. Poole. "On Measuring Partisanship in Roll-Call Voting: The U.S. House of Representatives, 1877–1999." *American Journal of Political Science* 46, no. 3 (July 2002): 477–89.

Craig, Maureen A., and Jennifer Richeson. "On the Precipice of a 'Majority-

Minority' America: Perceived Status Threat from the Racial Demographic Shift Affects White Americans' Political Ideology." *Psychological Science* 25, no. 6 (2014): 1189–97.

Crowder-Meyer, Melody Ara. "Local Parties, Local Candidates, and Women's Representation: How County Parties Affect Who Runs for and Wins Political Office." PhD diss., Princeton University, 2010.

Dahl, Robert Alan. *Dilemmas of Pluralist Democracy: Autonomy vs. control.* New Haven: Yale University Press, 1982.

Dalton, Russell J., David M. Farrell, and Ian McAllister. *Political Parties and Democratic Linkage: How Parties Organize Democracy.* New York: Oxford University Press, 2011.

Data Labs Team. *Partisan Conflict and Congressional Outreach.* Technical report. Pew Research Center, February 23, 2017. http://www.people-press.org/wp-content/uploads/sites/4/2017/02/LabsReport_FINALreport.pdf.

Desilver, Drew. *What Is the House Freedom Caucus, and Who's in It?* Technical report. Pew Research Center, October 20, 2015. Accessed March 14, 2019, and http://www.pewresearch.org/fact-tank/2015/10/20/house-freedom-caucus-what-is-it-and-whos-in-it/.

Diani, Mario, and Doug McAdam. *Social Movements and Networks: Relational Approaches to Collective Action.* New York: Oxford University Press, 2003.

DiSalvo, Daniel. *Engines of Change: Party Factions in American Politics, 1868–2010.* New York: Oxford University Press, 2012.

Disch, Lisa. "The Tea Party: A "White Citizenship" Movement?" *In Steep: The Precipitous Rise of the Tea Party,* edited by Lawrence Rosenthal and Christine Trost, 133–51. Berkeley: University of California Press, 2012.

Dombrink, John. *The Twilight of Social Conservatism: American Culture Wars in the Obama Era.* New York: NYU Press, 2015.

Dominguez, Casey B. K. "Groups and the Party Coalitions: A Network Analysis of Overlapping Donor Lists." American Political Science Association annual meeting paper, 2005.

Downs, Anthony. *An Economic Theory of Democracy.* New York: Harper, 1957.

Draper, Theodore. "Hume and Madison: The Secrets of Federalist Paper no. 10." *Encounter* 58, no. 34 (1982).

Ekins, Emily, and David Kirby. "Libertarian Roots of the Tea Party." *Cato Institute Policy Analysis* 705 (2012).

Fenno, Richard F. *Home Style: House Members in Their Districts.* New York: HarperCollins, 1978.

Ferrechio, Susan. "Libertarian Wing of GOP Gains Strength in Congress." *Washington Examiner,* January 24, 2014. Accessed March 16, 2019, at https://www.washingtonexaminer.com/libertarian-wing-of-gop-gains-strength-in-congress.

Fowler, James H. "Connecting the Congress: A Study of Cosponsorship Networks." *Political Analysis* 14, no. 4 (2006): 456–87.

———. "Legislative Cosponsorship Networks in the US House and Senate." *Social Networks* 28 (2006): 454–65.

Fredericks, Bob. "Ocasio-Cortez Pushes for a Leftist Revolt in the Democratic Party." *New York Post*, November 19, 2018. Accessed March 18, 2019, at https://nypost.com/2018/11/19/ocasio-cortez-pushes-for-a-leftist-revolt-in-the-democratic-party/.

Frederickson, Kari A. *The Dixiecrat Revolt and the End of the Solid South, 1932–1968.* Chapel Hill: University of North Carolina Press, 2001.

Freeman, Jo. "Resource Mobilization and Strategy: A Model for Analyzing Social Movement Organization Actions." In *The Dynamics of Social Movements*, edited by Mayer N. Zald and John D. McCarthy, 167–89. Cambridge, MA: Winthrop Publishers, 1979.

Gabbatt, Adam. "'Tea Party of the Left': Bernie Sanders' Ethos Endures in Impending Trump Era." *Guardian*, November 15, 2016. Accessed March 18, 2019, at https://www.theguardian.com/us-news/2016/nov/15/bernie-sanders-progressive-activism-trump-protests.

Galston, William A. "The Liberal Faction of the Democratic Party is Growing, New Polling Shows." Brookings, January 9, 2019. Accessed March 18, 2019, at https://www.brookings.edu/blog/fixgov/2019/01/11/the-liberal-faction-of-the-democratic-party-is-growing-new-polling-shows/.

Gamson, William A. *The Strategy of Social Protest.* Homewood, IL: Dorsey Press, 1975.

Garcia, Eric. "Lipinski Warns about Tea Party of the Left." *Roll Call*, March 5, 2018. Accessed March 18, 2019, at https://www.rollcall.com/news/politics/lipinski-warns-about-tea-party-of-the-left.

Gehrke, Joel. "Meet the Freedom Caucus." *National Review*, January 26, 2015. Accessed March 15, 2019, at https://www.nationalreview.com/2015/01/meet-freedom-caucus-joel-gehrke/.

Gervais, Bryan, and Irwin Morris. *Reactionary Republicanism: How the Tea Party in the House Paved the Way for Trump's Victory.* New York: Oxford University Press, 2018.

Gold, Matea. "How National Tea Party Groups Missed the David Brat Boat." *Washington Post*, June 19, 2014. Accessed March 15, 2019, at http://www.washingtonpost.com/blogs/the-fix/wp/2014/06/10/how-national-tea-party-groups-missed-the-david-brat-boat/.

Golshan, Tara, and Ella Nilsen. "Progressives in Congress Could Be the Tea Party of the Left." Vox, December 4, 2018. Accessed March 18, 2019, at https://www.vox.com/policy-and-politics/2018/12/4/18103476/progressives-congress-ocasio-cortez-freedom-caucus.

Gomez, Henry J. "Portage County Tea Party Leader Tom Zawistowski Launches

Bid to Be Next Ohio GOP Chairman." Cleveland.com, April 2, 2013. Accessed April 10, 2018, at http://www.cleveland.com/open/index.ssf/2013/04/%20portage_county_tea_party_ leade.html.

Good, Chris. "Signs of the Times: Slogans and Images from the Tea Party Rally." *Atlantic*, September 13, 2010. https://www.theatlantic.com/politics/archive/2010/09/signs-of-the-times-slogans-and-images-from-the-tea-partyrally/62885/.

Graham, David A. "How Far Have the Democrats Moved to the Left?" *Atlantic*, November 5, 2018. Accessed March 18, 2019, at https://www.theatlantic.com/politics/archive/2018/11/democratic-voters-move-leftward-range-issues/574834/.

Green, John C., and Daniel J. Coffey. *The State of the Parties: The Changing Role of Contemporary American Parties*. 6th. Edited by John C Green and Daniel J Coffey. Lanham, MD: Rowman & Littlefield, 2011.

Green, John C., Mark J. Rozell, and Clyde Wilcox. "Social Movements and Party Politics: The Case of the Christian Right." *Journal for the Scientific Study of Religion* 40, no. 3 (2001): 413–26.

Green, John Clifford, James L. Guth, and Corwin E. Smidt. *Religion and the Culture Wars: Dispatches from the Front*. Lanham, MD: Rowman & Littlefield, 1996.

Grimmer, Justin, and Gary King. "General Purpose Computer-Assisted Clustering and Conceptualization." *PNAS* 108, no. 7 (February 2011): 2643–50.

Grimmer, Justin, and Brandon M. Stewart. "Text as Data: The Promise and Pitfalls of Automatic Content Analysis Methods for Political Texts." *Political Analysis* 21, no. 3 (2013): 267–97.

Grimmer, Justin, Sean J. Westwood, and Solomon Messing. *The Impression of Influence: Legislator Communication, Representation, and Democratic Accountability*. Princeton, NJ: Princeton University Press, 2014.

Groseclose, Tim, and James M. Snyder. "Buying Supermajorities." *American Political Science Review* 90, no. 2 (1996): 303–15.

Grossmann, Matt, and Casey B. K. Dominguez. "Party Coalitions and Interest Group Networks." *American Politics Research* 37, no. 5 (2009): 767–800.

Gusfield, Joseph R. *Symbolic Crusade: Status Politics and the American Temperance Movement*. Champaign: University of Illinois Press, 1963.

Hall, Richard L., and Frank W. Wayman. "Buying Time: Moneyed Interests and the Mobilization of Bias in Congressional Committees." *American Political Science Review* 84, no. 3 (1990): 797–820.

Hamilton, Jacob. "Bernie Sanders Faces Two Big Challenges as He Enters the 2020 Race." NBC News, February 19, 2019. Accessed March 18, 2019, at https://www.nbcnews.com/politics/meet-the-press/bernie-sanders-faces-two-big-challenges-heenters-2020-race-n973006.

Hartman, Andrew. *A War for the Soul of America: A History of the Culture Wars*. Chicago: University of Chicago Press, 2015.

Heaney, Michael T., and Fabio Rojas. *Party in the Street: The Antiwar Movement and the Democratic Party after 9/11*. New York: Cambridge University Press, 2015.

Heflin, Jay. "Tea Party Primary Wins Give Boost to 'Fair Tax' Plan to Kill Federal Income Taxes." *The Hill*, September 20, 2010. Accessed September 1, 2019 at https://thehill.com/policy/finance/119655-tea-party-primary-wins-give -boost-to-fair-tax-reform-proposal.

Hemmer, Nicole. *Messengers of the Right: Conservative Media and the Transformation of American Politics*. Philadelphia: University of Pennsylvania Press, 2016.

Hershey, Marjorie. *Party Politics in America*. 17th edition. New York: Routledge, 2017.

Herszenhorn, David. "Congress Now Has a 'Tea Party Caucus.'" Caucus Blog of the *New York Times*, July 20, 2010. Accessed March 16, 2019, at https:// thecaucus.blogs.nytimes.com/2010/07/20/congress-now-has-a-tea-party-caucus/ ?mtrref=www.google.com&gwh=CEDAB5630C222434BF279F49C683B7AA &gwt=pay.

Hetherington, Marc J. "Resurgent Mass Partisanship: The Role of Elite Polarization." *American Political Science Review* 95, no. 3 (2001): 619–31.

Hofstadter, Richard. *The Paranoid Style in American Politics and Other Essays*. Cambridge, MA: Harvard University Press, 1965.

Hopkins, Daniel J. "The Exaggerated Life of Death Panels? The Limited but Real Influence of Elite Rhetoric in the 2009–2010 Health Care Debate." *Political Behavior* 40, no. 3 (2018): 681–709.

Hopkins, Daniel J., and Gary King. "A Method of Automated Nonparametric Content Analysis for Social Science." *American Journal of Political Science* 54, no. 1 (2009): 229–47.

Hopkins, David, and Matt Grossman. *Asymmetric Politics: Ideological Republicans and Group Interest Democrats*. New York: Oxford University Press, 2016.

———. "Ideological Republicans and Group Interest Democrats: The Asymmetry of American Party Politics." *Perspectives on Politics* 13, no. 1 (2015): 119–39.

Hume, David. *The History of England from the Invasion of Julius Caesar to the Revolution in 1688*, 6 vols. Indianapolis: Liberty Fund, 1983.

———. "Of the Coalition of Parties." In *On the Side of the Angels: An Appreciation of Parties and Partisanship*, edited by Nancy L Rosenblum, 122. Princeton, NJ: Princeton University Press, 2008.

Huston, Warner Todd. "AP Tars Tea Party Movement as 'Grandfathered' by Ron Paul." Publius Forum, May 4, 2011. Accessed April 10, 2018, at http://

www.chicagonow.com/publius-forum/2011/05/ap-tars-tea-party-movement
-as-grandfathered-by-ron-paul/.

Jacobson, Gary C. "Party Polarization in National Politics: The Electoral Connection." In *Polarized Politics: Congress and the President in a Partisan Era*, edited by Jon Bond and Richard Fleischer. Washington: Congressional Quarterly Press, 2000.

———. "The President, the Tea Party, and Voting Behavior in 2010: Insights from the Cooperative Congressional Election Study." APSA 2011 annual meeting paper, August 2011.

Jenkins, Jeffery A., Michael H. Crespin, and Jamie L. Carson. "Parties as Procedural Coalitions in Congress: An Examination of Differing Career Tracks." *Legislative Studies Quarterly* 30 (2005): 365–90.

Jessee, Stephen A., and Sean M. Theriault. "The Two Faces of Congressional Roll-Call Voting." *Party Politics* 20, no. 6 (October 2012): 836–48.

Jost, John T., Jack Glaser, Arie W. Kruglanski, and Frank J. Sulloway. "Political Conservatism as Motivated Social Cognition." *Psychological Bulletin* 129, no. 3 (2003): 339.

Judis, John, and Ruy Teixeira. *The Emerging Democratic Majority*. New York: Simon & Schuster, 2002.

Kabaservice, Geoffrey. *Rule and Ruin: The Downfall of Moderation and the Destruction of the Republican Party, from Eisenhower to the Tea Party*. New York: Oxford University Press, 2012.

Karol, David. *Party Position Change in American Politics: Coalition Management*. New York: Cambridge University Press, 2009.

Kaufman, Leslie, and Kate Zernike. "Activists Fight Green Projects, Seeing U.N. Plot." *New York Times*, February 3, 2012. Accessed March 14, 2019, at https://www.nytimes.com/2012/02/04/us/activists-fight-green-projects-seeing
-un-plot.html?mtrref=www.google.com&gwh=CFED7F74E2F8D0AB
3862E103381DBDA5&gwt=pay.

Kessler, Daniel, and Keith Krehbiel. "Dynamics of Cosponsorship." *American Political Science Review* 90, no. 3 (1996): 555–66.

Key, V. O. *Politics, Parties, and Pressure Groups*. 4th edition. New York: Thomas Y. Crowell Company, 1958.

King, Gayle. "Paul Ryan's Interview with *CBS This Morning* (Full Transcript)." CBS, April 12, 2018. Accessed March 15, 2019, at https://www.cbsnews.com/
news/paulryan-trump-stepping-down-cbs-interview-full-transcript-today
-2018–04–12/.

Klein, Ezra. "Eric Cantor Wasn't Beaten by the Tea Party." Vox, June 11, 2014. Accessed March 14, 2019, at https://www.vox.com/2014/6/11/5799710/Eric
-Cantor-beatentea-party.

Klein, Rick. "Democrats Seek to Own 'Occupy Wall Street' Movement." ABC

News, October 10, 2011. Accessed March 15, 2019, at https://abcnews.go.com/ Politics/democrats-seek-occupy-wall-street-movement/story?id=14701337.

Koger, Gregory. "Position Taking and Cosponsorship in the U.S. House." *Legislative Studies Quarterly* 28, no. 2 (May 2003): 225–46.

Koger, Gregory, Seth Masket, and Hans Noel. "Partisan Webs: Information Exchange and Party Networks." *British Journal of Political Science* 39, no. 3 (2009): 633–53.

Krebs, Valdis E. "Mapping Networks of Terrorist Cells." *Connections* 24, no. 3 (2002): 43–52.

Krutz, Glen S. "Issues and Institutions: "Winnowing" in the U.S. Congress." *American Journal of Political Science* 49, no. 2 (April 2005): 313–26.

Kumar, Anup. "The Tea Party Movement: The Problem of Populism as a Discursive Political Practice." *Javnost–The Public* 18, no. 4 (2011): 55–71.

Layman, Geoffrey. *The Great Divide: Religious and Cultural Conflict in American Party Politics*. New York: Columbia University Press, 2001.

Layman, Geoffrey C., Thomas Carsey, John Green, Richard Herrera, and Rosalyn Cooperman. "Activists and Conflict Extension in American Party Politics." *American Political Science Review*. 104, no. 2 (2010): 324–46.

Levendusky, Matthew. *The Partisan Sort: How Liberals Became Democrats and Conservatives Became Republicans*. Chicago: University of Chicago Press, 2009.

LeVine, Robert A., and Donald T Campbell. *Ethnocentrism: Theories of Conflict, Ethnic Attitudes, and Group Behavior*. Hoboken, NJ: John Wiley & Sons, 1972.

Lewis, Jeffrey B., Keith Poole, Howard Rosenthal, Adam Boche, Aaron Rudkin, and Luke Sonnet. Voteview: Congressional Roll-Call Votes Database. Voteview.com, 2018.

Libertarian Party. "Ohio Libertarians Get Coverage by Fielding Candidates." February 22, 2010. Accessed March 15, 2019, at https://www.lp.org/blogs-staff -ohio-libertarians-get-coverage-by-fielding-candidates/.

Lienesch, Michael. *In the Beginning: Fundamentalism, the Scopes Trial, and the Making of the Antievolution Movement*. H. Eugene and Lillian Youngs Lehman series. Chapel Hill: University of North Carolina Press, 2007.

Lipset, Seymour Martin, and Earl Raab. *The Politics of Unreason: Right Wing Extremism in America, 1790–1970*. New York: Harper & Row, 1978.

Lo, Clarence. "Astroturf versus Grass Roots: Scenes from Early Tea Party Mobilization." In *Steep: The Precipitous Rise of the Tea Party*, edited by Lawrence Rosenthal and Christine Trost. Berkeley: University of California Press, 2012.

MacWilliams, Matthew C. "Who Decides When the Party Doesn't: Authoritarian Voters and the Rise of Trump." *PS: Political Science and Politics* 29, no. 4 (2016): 716–21.

Madison, James. "Federalist No. 10." *New York Daily Advertiser*, 1787.

Major, Brenda, Alison Blodorn, and Gregory Major Blascovich. "The Threat of Increasing Diversity: Why Many White Americans Support Trump in the 2016 Presidential Election." *Group Processes and Intergroup Relations* 21, no. 6 (2018): 931–40.

Masket, Seth E. *No Middle Ground: How Informal Party Organizations Control Nominations and Polarize Legislatures*. Ann Arbor: University of Michigan Press, 2009.

Mason, Lilliana. "'I Disrespectfully Agree': The Differential Effects of Partisan Sorting on Social and Issue Polarization." *American Political Science Review* 59, no. 1 (2015): 128–45.

May, Henry Farnham. *The Enlightenment in America*. New York: Oxford University Press, 1976.

Mayhew, David R. *The Electoral Connection*. New Haven: Yale University Press, 2004.

———. *Placing Parties in American Politics: Organization, Electoral Settings, and Government Activity in the Twentieth Century*. Princeton, NJ: Princeton University Press, 1986.

McCarty, Nolan, Keith T. Poole, and Howard Rosenthal. "The Hunt for Party Discipline in Congress." *American Political Science Review* 95, no. 3 (September 2001): 673–87.

———. *Income Redistribution and the Realignment of American Politics*. Washington: AEI Press, 1997.

———. *Polarized America: The Dance of Ideology and Unequal Riches*. Cambridge, MA: MIT Press, 2008.

Mudde, Cas. "The Populist Zeitgeist." *Government and Opposition* 39 (2004).

Newhauser, Daniel. "What Happened to the Tea Party Caucus?" *Roll Call*, May 20, 2013. Accessed March 15, 2019, at https://www.rollcall.com/news/what_happened_to_the_tea_party_caucus-223309–1.html.

Noah, Timothy. "The Medicare-Isn't-Government Meme." Slate, August 5, 2009. https://slate.com/news-and-politics/2009/08/help-slate-track-the-medicareisn-t-government-meme.html.

Noel, Hans. *Political Ideologies and Political Parties in America*. New York: Cambridge University Press, 2013.

Noel, Hans, Seth E. Masket, and Gregory Koger. "Cooperative Party Factions in American Politics." *American Politics Research* 38, no. 1 (December 2009): 33–53.

Oldfield, Duane Murray. *The Right and the Righteous: The Christian Right Confronts the Republican Party*. Lanham, MD: Rowman & Littlefield, 1996.

Open Secrets. "Ohio Congressional Races 2010." 2010. Accessed April 10, 2018, at https://www.opensecrets.org/races/%20election?cycle=2010&id=KS04&state=OH.

———. "Virginia Congressional Races 2010." 2010. Accessed April 10, 2018, at https://www.opensecrets.%20org/races/election?cycle=2010&id=AK&state =VA.

Parker, Christopher S., and Matt A. Barreto. *Change They Can't Believe In: The Tea Party and Reactionary Politics in America*. Princeton, NJ: Princeton University Press, 2013.

Pelinka, Anton. "Right-Wing Populism: Concept and Typology." In *Right-Wing Populism in Europe: Politics and Discourse*, edited by Ruth Wodak, Majid Khosravinik, and Brigitte Mral. New York: Bloomsbury, 2013.

Petrocik, John R. "Realignment: New Party Coalitions and the Nationalization of the South." *Journal of Politics* 49, no. 2 (1987): 347–75.

Polsby, Nelson W. *Consequences of Party Reform*. New York: Oxford University Press, 1983.

Pons, Pascal, and Matthieu Latapy. "Computing Communities in Large Networks Using Random Walks." *Journal of Graph Algorithms Applications* 10, no. 2 (2006): 191–218.

Poole, Keith T., and Howard Rosenthal. *Congress: A Political-Economic History of Roll Call Voting*. New York: Oxford University Press, 1997.

———. "The Polarization of American Politics." *Journal of Politics*. 46, no. 4 (1984): 1061–79.

Ranney, J. Austin. *Curing the Mischiefs of Faction: Party Reform in America*. Berkeley: University of California Press, 1975.

Religion and Politics. *The Tea Party and Religion*. Technical report. Pew Research Center, February 23, 2011. http://www.pewforum.org/2011/02/23/tea -party-and-religion/.

Reynolds, Michael. "Photo Essay: Signs of the Tea-Party Protests." *Time*. Accessed March 18, 2019, at http://content.time.com/time/photogallery/0,29307 ,1922169,00.html.

Ringe, Nils, Jennifer Nicoll Victor, and Christopher J. Carman. *Bridging the Information Gap: Legislative Member Organizations as Social Networks in the United States and the European Union*. Ann Arbor: University of Michigan Press, 2013.

"The Rise of the LPVA." Virginia Conservative, June 19, 2014. Accessed April 10, 2018, at http://virginiaconservative.net/tag/stuart-bain.

Roberts, Margaret E., Brandon Stewart, and Dustin Tingley. "stm: R Package for Structural Topic Models." *Journal of Statistical Software* 10, no. 2 (2018).

Rohde, David W. *Parties and Leaders in the Postreform House*. Chicago: University of Chicago Press, 1991.

Rohde, David, and Michael H. Crespin. *Political Institutions and Public Choice Roll-Call Database*. Technical report. Norman, OK: Carl Albert Center, University of Oklahoma, 2017.

Rosenblum, Nancy L. *On the Side of the Angels: An Appreciation of Parties and Partisanship*. Princeton, NJ: Princeton University Press, 2008.

Rosenstone, Steven J., Roy Behr, and Edward H. Lazarus. *Third Parties in America: Citizen Response to Major Party Failure*. Princeton, NJ: Princeton University Press, 1984.

Rubin, Ruth Bloch. *Building the Bloc: Intraparty Organization in the US Congress*. New York: Cambridge University Press, 2017.

Sabato, Larry J., Kyle Kondik, and Geoffrey Skelley. "So What Just Happened in Virginia? A Brief History of Old Dominion Nomination Battles." University of Virginia Center for Politics, May 2013. Accessed May 1, 2018, at http://www.centerforpolitics.org/crystalball/articles/are-primaries-or-conventions-more-successful-for-a-party/.

Sartori, Giovanni. *Parties and Party Systems: A Framework for Analysis*. New York: Cambridge University Press, 1976.

Schattschneider, Elmer Eric. *Party Government*. New York: Holt, Rinehart & Winston, 1942.

Schickler, Eric. *Disjointed Pluralism: Institutional Innovation and the Development of the U.S. Congress*. Princeton, NJ: Princeton University Press, 2001.

Schlozman, Daniel. *When Movements Anchor Parties: Electoral Alignments in American History*. Princeton, NJ: Princeton University Press, 2015.

Schwartz, Mildred A. *The Party Network: The Robust Organization of Illinois Republicans*. Madison: University of Wisconsin Press, 1990.

Sessions, David. "Tea Party: Is It the Christian Right in Disguise?" Daily Beast, August 8, 2011. Accessed March 15, 2019, at https://www.thedailybeast.com/tea-party-is-it-the-christian-right-in-disguise.

Shepard, Alex. "It's Not Bernie Sanders's Job to Unify the Democratic Party." *New Republic*, May 20, 2016. Accessed March 15, 2019, at https://newrepublic.com/article/133642/its-not-bernie-sanderss-job-unify-democratic-party.

Shepard, Steven. "Poll: Majority of Voters Back Trump Travel Ban." Politico, July 5, 2017. Accessed March 10, 2019, at https://www.politico.com/story/2017/07/05/trumptravel-ban-poll-voters-240215.

Sherman, Jake. "Bachmann Forms Tea Party Caucus." Politico, July 16, 2010. Accessed March 16, 2019, at https://www.politico.com/story/2010/07/bachmann-forms-teaparty-caucus-039848.

Sides, John, Michael Tesler, and Lynn Vavrek. *Identity Crisis: The 2016 Presidential Campaign and the Battle for the Meaning of America*. Princeton, NJ: Princeton University Press, 2018.

Sinclair, Barbara. *Party Wars: Polarization and the Politics of National Policy Making*. Norman: University of Oklahoma Press, 2014.

Skinner, Richard M. "Do 527s Add Up to a Party? Thinking about the "Shadows" of Politics." *The Forum* 3, no. 3 (2005).

Skocpol, Theda, and Alexander Hertel-Fernandez. "The Koch Network and Republican Party Extremism." *Perspectives on Politics* 14, no. 3 (2016): 681–99.

Smyth, Julie Carr. "Federal Judge Upholds Third-Party Ballot Rules in Ohio." *Akron Beacon Journal*, April 16, 2015. Accessed April 10, 2018, at https://www.ohio.com/akron/news/federal-judge-upholds-third-party-ballot-rules-in-ohio.

Snyder, James M., Stephen Ansolabehere, and C. Stewart. "The Effects of Party and Preferences on Congressional Roll Call Voting." *Legislative Studies Quarterly* 26, no. 4 (2001): 533–72.

Snyder, James M., and Tim Groseclose. "Estimating Party Influence in Congressional Roll-Call Voting." *American Journal of Political Science* 44, no. 2 (2000): 193–211.

Spencer, Mark G. "Hume and Madison on Faction." *William and Mary Quarterly* 59, no. 4 (2002): 869–96.

Staniland, Paul. *Networks of Rebellion: Explaining Insurgent Cohesion and Collapse*. Ithaca, NY: Cornell University Press, 2014.

Stelter, Brian. "CNBC Replays Its Reporter's Tirade." *New York Times*, February 22, 2009. Accessed July 30, 2019, at https://www.nytimes.com/2009/02/23/business/media/23cnbc.html.

Stewart, Martina. "Tea Party Groups Target Senate after Presidential 'Disappointments.'" CNN, March 29, 2012. Accessed March 1, 2019, at https://www.cnn.com/2012/03/29/politics/tea-party-election/index.html.

Stokes, Susan C. "Political Parties and Democracy." *Annual Review of Political Science* 2, no. 1 (1999): 243–67.

Sundquist, James L. *Dynamics of the Party System*. Washington: Brookings Institution, 1983.

Tam Cho, Wendy K., and James H. Fowler. "Legislative Success in a Small World: Social Network Analysis and the Dynamics of Congressional Legislation." *Journal of Politics* 72, no. 1 (2010): 124–35.

Theriault, Sean M. *The Gingrich Senators: The Roots of Partisan Warfare in Congress*. Oxford University Press, 2013.

———. *Party Polarization in Congress*. New York: Cambridge University Press, 2008.

Victor, Jennifer Nicoll. "Can Congress Build Bipartisanship through Caucuses?" The Conversation, September 14, 2016. Accessed March 15, 2019, at https://theconversation.com/can-congress-build-bipartisanship-through-caucuses-64286.

Victor, Jennifer Nicoll, and Gregory Koger. "Financing Friends: How Lobbyists Create a Web of Relationships among Members of Congress." *Interest Groups & Advocacy* 5, no. 3 (May 2016): 224–62.

Virginia Department of Elections. "Political Party Committees." Accessed

March 15, 2018, at https://www.elections.virginia.gov/candidatepac-info/
political-committees/political-party-committees/.

Vozzella, Laura. "Virginia GOP Picks Staunch Conservatives as Statewide Candidates." *Washington Post*, May 19, 2013. https://www.washingtonpost.com/
local/va-politics/virginia-gop-picks-staunch-conservatives-as-statewide
-candidates/2013/05/18/138040b4-bef7–11e2–89c9–3be8095fe767_story.
html?utm_term=.113d9694872e.

Walker, Jack L. *Mobilizing Interest Groups in America: Patrons, Professions,
and Social Movements*. Ann Arbor: University of Michigan Press, 1991.

Warren, James. "Warren: House Majority Leader Eric Cantor's Defeat Shows
Tea Party Is Not Dead." *New York Daily News*, June 11, 2014. Accessed
March 18, 2019, at https://www.nydailynews.com/news/politics/warren-eric
-cantor-defeat-shows-tea-party-not-dead-article-1.1824965?barcprox=true.

Wasserman, David. *Introducing the 2012 Cook Political Report Partisan Voter
Index*. Technical report. Cook Political Report, October 11, 2012.

Wilcox, Clyde, and Carin Robinson. *Onward Christian Soldiers? The Religious
Right in American Politics*. New York: Routledge, 2011.

Williamson, Vanessa. "What the Tea Party Tells Us about the Trump Presidency."
Brookings Institution. November 2016. Accessed September 15, 2019, at https://
www.brookings.edu/blog/fixgov/2016/11/09/tea-party-and-trump-presidency/.

Williamson, Vanessa, and Theda Skocpol. *The Tea Party and the Remaking of
Republican Conservatism*. Revised edition. New York: Oxford University
Press, 2016.

Wilson, Reid. "The Three Republican Lanes: Establishment, Values, Change."
Morning Consult, February 20, 2016. Accessed March 14, 2019, at https://
morningconsult.com/2016/02/20/the-three-republican-lanes-establishment
-values-change/.

Wilson, Rick K., and Cheryl D. Young. "Cosponsorship in the U.S. Congress."
Legislative Studies Quarterly 22, no. 1 (February 1997): 25–43.

Woon, Jonathan. "Bill Sponsorship in Congress: The Moderating Effect of
Agenda Positions on Legislative Proposals." *Journal of Politics* 70, no. 1
(2008): 201–16.

Zernike, Kate. *Boiling Mad: Inside Tea Party America*. New York: MacMillan,
2010.

Index

CPSIA information can be obtained
at www.ICGtesting.com
Printed in the USA
LVHW081541150921
697891LV00002B/315